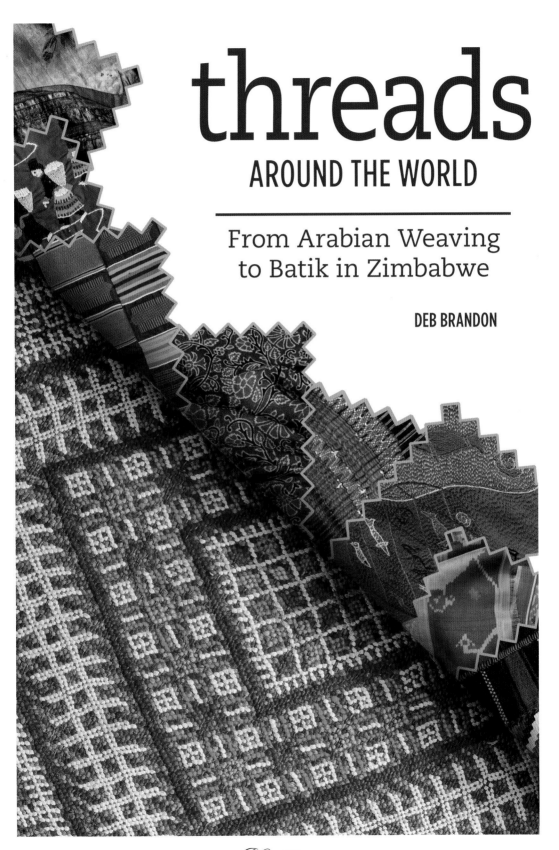

threads

AROUND THE WORLD

From Arabian Weaving
to Batik in Zimbabwe

DEB BRANDON

4880 Lower Valley Road • Atglen, PA 19310

Other Schiffer Books on Related Subjects:

Cotton & Indigo from Japan, Teresa Duryea Wong, ISBN 978-0-7643-5351-2

Andean Sling Braids: New Designs for Textile Artists, Rodrick Owen & Terry Newhouse Flynn, ISBN 978-0-7643-5103-7

Norwegian Pick-Up Bandweaving, Heather Torgenrud, ISBN 978-0-7643-4751-1

Designed by Molly Shields
Cover design by Ro S
Front cover images by Joe Coca
Type set in Caecilia LT Std/Cambria

ISBN: 978-0-7643-5650-6
Printed in China

Published by Schiffer Publishing, Ltd.
4880 Lower Valley Road
Atglen, PA 19310
Phone: (610) 593-1777; Fax: (610) 593-2002
E-mail: Info@schifferbooks.com
Web: www.schifferbooks.com

For our complete selection of fine books on this and related subjects, please visit our website at www.schifferbooks.com. You may also write for a free catalog.

Schiffer Publishing's titles are available at special discounts for bulk purchases for sales promotions or premiums. Special editions, including personalized covers, corporate imprints, and excerpts, can be created in large quantities for special needs. For more information, contact the publisher.

We are always looking for people to write books on new and related subjects. If you have an idea for a book, please contact us at proposals@schifferbooks.com.

Photo courtesy of Prof. Ravi Poovaiah and Roopa Narayan Sahoo, D'source (E-kalpa Project)

Dedicated to my tribe

Photo courtesy of Estan Cabigas

CONTENTS

ACKNOWLEDGMENTS

First, I'd like to thank the team at Schiffer Publishing for helping me release this book into the world, especially Pete Schiffer and Sandra Korinchak. I am also grateful to Judy Fort Brenneman, my writing coach, editor, and close friend, for her help in transforming a grassroots project into a publish-worthy book.

I feel very fortunate to have worked with the amazing textile photographer Joe Coca, whose fabulous photos lifted this book far above what I thought possible. Thanks also to graphic designer Shawna Turner for her talents, Brendan Wiant for his organizational savvy and image research, Steve Csipke for indexing, and all those wonderful people who generously shared their photos of artists and artisans.

I also want to acknowledge textile artisans across the globe for keeping their traditions alive, reminding us that we all are connected though time and space. We all are made of the same cloth.

And my eternal gratitude to WARP and its members, my tribe, for setting me on this road. I am awestruck every day by your dedication. Without you, this book would not exist.

Photo courtesy of Joe Coca

INTRODUCTION

As I weave a textile, every so often pausing to gaze at the emerging patterns, I feel as if I am breathing life into it, and when I free it from the loom, I am releasing it into the world as a living entity—a textile is born, with a story yet to be told.

I look around me at the textiles I cherish, and I see ongoing stories. I see life.

The first wall hanging I wove reminds me of the weeks I spent learning to weave, the beginning of a passion for textiles, and a friendship with my teacher. My felt rug lay on the floor of a yurt before it came to my home; its wear and tear are the result of years of use by its creators, Mongolian nomads. I trace the pattern on my flatwoven cushion cover from the Middle Atlas of Morocco, recalling the stories another friend told me of her times with the Berber weavers and the beautiful textiles they create.

I've been surrounded by handmade ethnic textiles since my early childhood. The rugs on our cold tile floors at home were handwoven, and the cut pile carpet in the living room was hand knotted. My parents purchased the covers for the cushions that were scattered throughout our house in the nearby Druze village, and the donkey saddlebags I used to carry my books in high school were Bedouin woven.

I started dabbling in the textile arts around the age of seven, when my mother taught me to knit. I moved on to sewing patches on my brothers' jeans, embroidering flowers to cover stains on T-shirts, sewing clothing for my sister and myself, and knitting socks and sweaters.

After the terrorist attacks of September 11, 2001, feeling the need to actively work toward a better world, I joined WARP (Weave a Real Peace), a nonprofit networking organization whose members are dedicated to improving the quality of life of textile artisans in communities in need via their textile traditions. Growing up in Israel, through several wars, in an academic household, led me to the conviction that only through education and knowledge can humanity resolve our cultural differences. Weave a Real Peace lends me access to like-minded people—WARP members also feel they can make a difference in the world through textiles, and many of us act on this belief.

In 2003, I began writing articles for WARP's quarterly newsletter. Linda Temple, the editor, named my column "Textile Techniques from around the World."

Writing these articles has enriched my life and my weaving immeasurably. Though often limited to traveling vicariously through friends and relatives, I take great joy in traveling virtually through the research I conduct for the articles. In my explorations, I have sought out opportunities to talk to textile artists from around the world, with whom I communicate regularly.

Learning about far-flung cultures and techniques has enhanced my own textile creations too, as I borrow and adapt techniques and symbols, from sadza batik from Zimbabwe to weaving a skirt fashioned after Palestinian embroidery or knitting a gray-and-white hat in a Norwegian pattern. I hope that my passion for these textile traditions is contagious, and that you, too, will feel that your life has been enriched.

Textiles are an integral part of the human condition, weaving into the fabric of our being. Traditional textiles help us maintain our connections between past and present and our ties to each other. They prevent us from losing our humanity. We must keep textile traditions alive; we must nourish them.

Through the years, I have researched and written about more than fifty different textile techniques. In 2006, Linda Temple suggested putting all of the articles together in one publication that would be available to WARP members and all others interested in "Textile Techniques from around the World," as a fundraiser for WARP.

The project grew and evolved over the next ten years. Instead of our original plan of simply reprinting the articles, each accompanied with photos taken by WARP members during their travels, I rewrote, enriched, and expanded a subset of the entire collection, focusing less on the mechanics of the techniques and more on their stories. At the end of each chapter, I included a list of the resources I found helpful, for those who want to learn more. Along the way, I worked with editor Judy Fort Brenneman, and with the renowned textile photographer Joe Coca.

More than a decade after the initial idea, I'm proud to present this collection for you to enjoy.

CHAPTER 1

Morocco

Berber Flatweave

To the Berber, weaving is life.

The lifespan begins as the weaver prepares the loom for weaving and ends when she cuts the finished textile off the loom.

When I first learned of the Berber view, the notion of associating the finished textile with death filled me with unease. I couldn't accept it; when *I* set my scissors to the fabric, I am giving birth to it, sending it off into the world.

There had to be more to this belief, and I discovered there is. To the Berber, death is followed by an afterlife: when the completed textile enters its home, it is reborn to begin life anew.

The Berber identify the wool, the loom, and the act of weaving with matters of fertility and motherhood. The weaving is a metaphor for the evolving relationship between mother and son in a male-dominated society.

Preparing the upright (vertical) loom for weaving includes setting up the frame, winding the warp, and warping; that is, attaching the warp threads to the upper and lower beams. This process represents the years when a boy lives among the women, under his mother's protection and supervision.

The act of mounting the beams on the loom symbolizes his passage into adulthood. Berber society views a child as male only anatomically until his circumcision, which is when he acquires a male identity and takes his place among the Berber men. Analogous to a boy's coming of age, when the weft first crosses the warp, the textile also acquires a *ruh*, a soul.

The weaving itself, passing the shuttle to and fro across the warp threads, represents the journey of a mature male through life. The beginning of the weaving

embodies a young man's foray into the world, away from his mother's sphere of influence. Weaving can be unpredictable, despite the weaver's best intentions; so is a man's journey through adulthood into old age, despite his upbringing. Berber weavers associate difficulties in weaving, such as broken warp threads or a delay in progress, with mishaps along a man's path in life.

Finally, the textile "dies" when the weaver completes it. In the same way the Berber perform funeral rites for a man who has completed his journey through life, the weaver prepares the textile for its next phase, life after death, or the afterlife in Islam. Before the weaver removes it from the loom, she daubs the textile with salt water and recites the first pillar of Islam ("There is no God but Allah and Mohammad is his prophet") three times.

The dead pass into the afterlife, and the Berber textile passes into a new life, a form of rebirth. When it enters its new home, the Berber rug acquires a new *ruh*, a new soul for a new beginning.

The Berber tribes are indigenous to North Africa. Many of those living in rural areas have maintained their ethnic identity, despite the eighth-century Arab invasion and subsequent conversion to Islam.

Unlike the men, Berber women usually stay close to home and are therefore less exposed to outside influences. Consequently, the women are instrumental in propagat-

    Photos courtesy of Susan Schaefer Davis

ing the Berber linguistic and cultural heritage. Weaving and its traditions remain central to the lives of Berber women, who continue to pass these traditions down from mother to daughter.

Berber women weave a variety both of flatweave and knotted-pile rugs. Despite increasing intrusion from the outside world, it is still possible to determine the geographical origin and tribal affiliation of many Berber textiles through the weaving techniques, patterns, and embellishments.

The Berbers of the High Atlas Mountains are settled farmers; the tribes of the Middle Atlas are traditionally nomads or seminomadic. Possibly due to differences in lifestyle and environment, both the techniques and the patterns of their flatwoven textiles are quite distinct.

The flatwoven rugs of the Middle Atlas, called *hnabel* (singular *hanbel*), have floats in the back. The flatwoven textiles of the High Atlas have no floats and are completely reversible.

Both in the High Atlas and the Middle Atlas, the building blocks of the traditional patterns are simple geometric designs. Motifs include diamonds, triangles, herringbones, zigzags, and checkerboards, in many cases symbolizing aspects of fertility, such as male and female genitalia, conception, and birth.

There are distinct regional differences in arranging these motifs. Rugs of the High Atlas have clear centers and well-defined borders or frames. The traditional rugs of the Middle Atlas nomads are usually patterned in selvedge-to-selvedge stripes, with no distinct center or borders.

The simplest designs incorporate single-colored strips only. The more complex pieces alternate single-colored bands with patterned bands. As has been the case for hundreds of years, it is still possible in today's Berber flatwoven rugs to identify the tribal affiliation of the Berber weaver by studying the combination of colors, ratio of patterned to simple bands, width of the stripes, and the complexity and intricacy of the designs.

The abundant use of a variety of shades of red combined with dense and detailed patterns characterize many of the Zemmour tribe's pieces. Rugs from the Zayan tribe are similar to the Zemmour but are more colorful. The stripes are wider, the patterned stripes are farther apart, and the designs are larger and bolder.

The Beni Ouarain tribe uses flatweave for the women's shawls, where the single color stripes, which are often white, are relatively sparse. Most of the stripes are finely patterned in black and white, and usually no two patterned stripes are alike.

Middle Atlas flatweave artisans often incorporate additional decorative elements into their rugs, pillows, and shawls—tucking tufts of wool into some of the stripes during the weaving process, for example. Also, many Berber weavers of the Middle Atlas sew shiny sequins onto their flatwoven pieces, adding sparkle to the textiles.

The chedwi rug, woven by the Berber of the Siroua Mountain in the High Atlas, holds a unique position among the Berber flatweaves. Long and narrow, mostly black and white, the chedwis are, like the sequined rugs of the Middle Atlas, easy to spot from afar. But their most striking distinction is in the actual weaving process; chedwis combine three different weaving techniques: selvedge-to-selvedge plain weave, tapestry, and twining.

The word *chedwi* means twining, a method that involves enclosing individual warp threads across the width of a rug by twisting two strands of weft yarn around each warp thread in a figure eight. Chedwi weavers achieve spectacular twill-like designs by twisting the strands once or twice in repeating patterns. If the strands are of different colors, one black, the other white, twisting them once will alternate the colors across warp threads. If instead the

Photo courtesy of Susan Schaefer Davis

weaver twists the strands twice around each other before enclosing the next warp thread, the colors won't alternate.

Some of the plain-weave stripes are of one color, black or white, and others are patterned. The patterned strips, combining various geometric shapes, mostly in black and white, can also include colored yarn. Tapestry techniques enter into the weaving in patterned parts that include large single-colored areas, where there is a separate weft for each differently colored area.

A finished chedwi consists of strips of twining alternating with strips of weft-faced plain weave (where the warp hides beneath the weft). As a result, chedwis do not always lie completely flat on an even floor—it is not easy to maintain an even tension on the warp when using more than one weaving method within a single textile.

I gaze at my hanbel from the Middle Atlas, a collector's item, its colors no longer bright, and see it as a source of stories that bring it to life.

I trace the pattern and think of its maker. As she wove it, did she think fondly of her son, now a man, an outsider to her world? Did she marvel at the patterns and colors as they emerged, as I now marvel at her weaving prowess?

Resources

Barbattie, Bruno. *Berber Carpets of Morocco: The Symbols, Origin and Meaning.* Translated by Alan J. Bridgeman. Paris: Art Creation Realisation, 2008.

Davis, Susan Schaefer. *Patience and Power: Women's Lives in a Moroccan Village.* Rochester, VT: Schenkman Books, 1982.

Davis, Susan Schaefer. Anthropologist and WARP member, private communication, 2011–2017.

Fiske, Patricia L., W. Russell Pickering, and Ralph Y. Yoshe, eds. *From the Far West: Carpets and Textiles of Morocco.* Washington, DC: Textile Museum, 1980.

Messick, Brinkley. "Subordinate Discourse: Women, Weaving, and Gender Relations in North Africa." *American Ethnologist* 14, no. 2 (1987): 210–225.

Paydar, Niloo Imami, and Ivo Grammet, eds. *The Fabric of Moroccan Life.* Indianapolis, IN: Indianapolis Museum of Art, 2002.

CHAPTER 2

Hungary
Matyó Embroidery

We crowded around Dad as he rummaged through his suitcase for presents. I must have been eight or nine years old. He pulled out a blue piece of fabric and turned toward me. He shook it out—a "me-sized" apron, saturated with embroidery, large flowers in brilliant colors—and said, "It's from Hungary."

Matyó embroidery, with its large floral designs in vivid colors, is the type of embroidery that we most commonly associate with Hungarian folk art. Collectors don't measure the skill of the embroiderers in their ability to yield fine, intricate details, but in the evenness, regularity, and density of the stitching, the sharpness of the images, and the overall design and color combinations. The artists usually work with heavy cotton or wool thread and use satin stitch to fill in the flowers and leaves. Matyó embroiderers typically ply their art on cotton, linen, or wool fabric for their traditional dress and linens.

I recently purchased a cotton Matyó embroidered pillowcase (shown at left). Though it is lovely and skillfully made, buying it was a bit of a compromise on my part. I would have preferred a more densely embroidered textile, perhaps with a black background rather than white. But the pieces I truly covet are the traditional, richly embroidered sheepskin jackets and cloaks that I can only afford to admire from afar.

Traditional Matyó embroidery incorporates components of European Renaissance and baroque styles, as well as Turkish and Persian elements. The overall symmetry and the interplay between tendrils of foliage and the flower heads are European inspired. The Middle Eastern impact is evident in the asymmetry in the

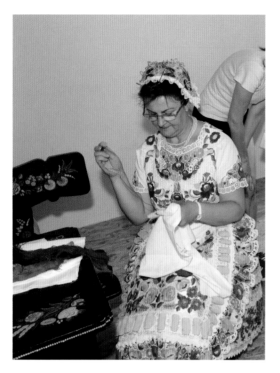

details and the stylized images of tulips, roses, carnations, and pomegranates.

During the Middle Ages, the Hungarian aristocracy prized Matyó embroidery. Many noblemen supported master embroiderers, in some cases founding embroidery workshops on their estates, where young girls could learn the craft and embellish the textiles of the estate. In comparison to the embroidery designated for Hungarian nobles, folk embroidery was less stylized, with designs that were more free-form.

In the late 1800s and early 1900s, Matyó embroidery caught the attention of the arts-and-crafts circles in Europe, especially in Britain. Could Dad have bought my apron in England? Surely not; like me, he is a bit of an authenticity snob. I just can't see him purchasing it anywhere other than Hungary. I suspect he didn't stray far out of his way to buy my apron. Did he find it while in Budapest for a conference? It certainly wasn't one of the mass-produced knockoffs of Matyó embroidery currently sold in Europe—mine, though not one of the finer pieces, was a genuine example of Matyó hand embroidery.

To purchase an authentic piece of fine Matyó embroidery, a collector is best off going straight to the source—Mezôkövesd, a town in northeastern Hungary, where there is a large concentration of the Matyó people (a Magyar-speaking Hungarian ethnic group). Or even better, go to the villages in the surrounding area, where you can meet still more Matyó artists in person.

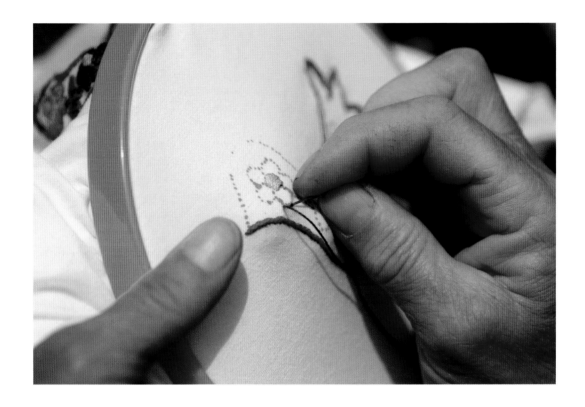

Resources

Gillow, John, and Bryan Sentance. *World Textiles: A Visual Guide to Traditional Techniques*. New York: Thames & Hudson, 1999.

Kubilius, Kerry. "Hungarian Culture." *TripSavvy* (blog), http://goeasteurope.about.com/od/hungary/a/Hungarian-Matyo-Folk-Art.htm.

Leslie, Catherine Amoroso. *Needlework through History: An Encyclopedia*. Westport, CT: Greenwood, 2007.

Paine, Sheila. *Embroidered Textiles*. New York: Thames & Hudson, 1990.

BASS

B Singer

CHAPTER 3

Japan
Gyotaku (Fish Printing)

Our instructor dumped a cooler full of freshly caught fish on the floor. My daughter, Sarah, sent me over to choose our fish. She wanted no part in the slimy portion of the process.

Before my daughter realized that participating in joint activities with me was supposed to be embarrassing, I often perused newsletters from the Pittsburgh Center for the Arts and the Boyd Community Center, searching for opportunities to dabble in crafts that would interest us both. We attended classes on jewelry making, glassblowing, and my personal favorite, gyotaku, Japanese fish printing. *Gyo* means "fish," and *taku* means "rubbing."

There are two theories about the origins of the art of fish printing. One attributes its invention to samurai warriors some time around the 1700s. The art of gyotaku not only exhibited their fishing prowess, but also their artistic skills. The second theory is that Catholic priests interested in gravestone rubbing introduced the art to Japan around 1855. Though it may not be clear how gyotaku came into being, there is no doubt that it was the method Japanese fishermen practiced to record their catch as far back as the 1800s.

Traditionally, fishermen used black carbon sumi inks on rice paper or on silk fabric. The inks were nontoxic and easy to wash off—after the printing, the fish were safe to eat.

Fish printing is not for the squeamish. Preparation for the printing includes cleaning freshly caught fish to remove bodily fluids, then sealing the various orifices to prevent leakage. The next step involves laying the fish on a flat surface and spreading and anchoring the fins and tail. Many artists prop the mouth open as well. As I worked with Sarah on our fish, I delighted in the "eews" I evoked from her.

Photos courtesy of Barry Singer, fishfanatic.etsy.com

There are two methods of fish printing. The traditional technique in Japan is the indirect method, which is reminiscent of stone rubbing. The artist places paper over the fish, dips a silk tampo (a cotton ball wrapped in silk) in ink, then dabs the paper with it. When using the direct method, the artist applies ink to the surface of the clean fish, then places the paper (or fabric) on top of the painted fish, and rubs gently to transfer the ink from the fish to the underside of the paper. The indirect method is easier to control and yields a slightly abstracted result, and the direct method produces bold prints with strong details.

During the printing process, gyotaku artists leave the eyes blank. In the last step, the artist brings the print to life by painting a band of colored iris around a large black pupil, and a glint of white—thus "returning the spirit" of the fish.

Gyotaku has become very popular in the US in the last three decades, often decorating T-shirts and bags. In the class Sarah and I took, using the direct method, we brushed the fish with acrylic paints. We found that no matter how bold our colors, the print didn't come alive until we touched the iris with a flash of white—it was magical. We did indeed return the spirit of the fish.

Resources

Dahl, Carolyn A. *Natural Impressions: Taking an Artistic Path through Nature.* New York: Watson-Guptill, 2002.

Dahl, Carolyn A. *Transforming Fabric: 30 Creative Ways to Paint, Dye, and Pattern Cloth.* Iola, WI: Krause, 2004.

Laury, Jean Ray. *Imagery on Fabric: A Complete Surface Design Handbook.* Concord, CA: C&T Publishing, 1997.

Singer, Barry. Gyotaku artist, etsy.com/shop/fishfanatic.

CHAPTER 4

China

Miao Shiny Cloth

Flipping through Sadae and Tomoko Torimaru's book *Imprints on Cloth*, I was struck by a photo of a Miao woman carrying her baby—the indigo-dyed carrier was soaking wet. Then I noticed that an elderly gentleman in another photo was wearing a wet, indigo-dyed jacket.

Both the woman and the elderly gentleman were Blue Hmong, a subgroup of the Miao of China. What seemed to be wet fabric was, in fact, glossy, indigo-dyed fabric that is highly valued among the Blue Hmong.

Many Blue Hmong reside in Thailand, Vietnam, Laos, and Burma, but the majority live in southwestern China, in Guizhou Province.

Indigo dyeing is not uncommon among ethnic groups around the world; different plants from across the globe yield the same magical dyeing experience. But the Blue Hmong take indigo dyeing to another level—they produce an indigo-dyed fabric with a startling sheen to it.

The method of achieving the sheen differs from location to location, family to family, and artisan to artisan. The various methods usually include immersion or coating in a starchy solution, or a glaze, and repeated pounding.

In Gedong, in northeastern Guizhou, after indigo-dyeing a piece of fabric, the artisans soak it in a vat of yellow bean juice. Next, they pound the dried fabric with a heavy wooden mallet, then steam it, indigo-dye it again, and then soak it in wild walnut juice. They repeat the process several times. In the next phase, they soak it in an extract of water-buffalo skin and dry it. The last step involves dyeing the fabric once more, rinsing it, and, finally, pounding it one last time.

Photo courtesy of Pamela Najdowski

Instead of soaking the fabric, the Danzhai dyers in southwestern Guizhou coat it with pig's blood. In Tingdong, the dyers coat the dyed fabric with a mixture of beaten egg whites and medicinal herbs, and in Rongjiang, they make a glaze out of indigo dye paste and the glue-like juice from unripe persimmons.

In Gulong, in southeastern Guizhou, they smoke dyed cloth over burning Chinese juniper to bring out the desired color. The soot, which clings to the fabric, brings gloss to the fabric after a good beating.

Some artisans in southern Guizhou do not pound the fabric with a wooden mallet; instead they use a huge, arc-shaped stone. The artisans wind the dyed fabric around a roller, place the stone on top, and then rock the stone arc, either by hand or by standing on the stone and shifting their weight side to side.

There are no shortcuts in any of the methods. Each one is a long, laborious

Photo courtesy of Serena Lee, Textile Odyssey Tours, textileodyssey.com

process, lasting several days. Each one produces the same stunning result: indigo-dyed fabric so glossy that at first glance it may appear to be soaking wet.

I finally had the opportunity to see up-close a couple of shiny, indigo-dyed jackets from Guizhou.

I was not surprised to find that both were stiff. I was, however, surprised by the depth the shine lent to the fabric, bringing it to life. One piece, shown on page 28, was a deep green, and its color varied with the light, even sometimes featuring a yellow/brown sheen. The other jacket shone in a fathomless dark blue, and the color transformed with the light, from black to yellow and a deep green. Spectacular!

Resources

Corrigan, Gina. *Miao Textiles from China*. Seattle: University of Washington Press, 2001.

Torimaru, Sadae, and Tomoko Torimaru. *Imprints on Cloth: 18 Years of Research among the Miao People of Guizhou, China*. Translated by Yoshiko I. Wada and Nancy Salumbides. Fukuoka, Japan: Akishige Tada, 2004.

Torimaru, Tomoko. *One Needle, One Thread: Miao (Hmong) Embroidery and Fabric Piecework from Guizhou, China*. Honolulu: University of Hawai'i Art Gallery, 2008.

CHAPTER 5

Pakistan

Ajrakh Block Printing

My brothers pooled their resources to buy me a gift for my first wedding: an antique bedspread from Persia, block-printed with rows and rows of turbaned horseback riders. Wherever I go, it goes, as a wall hanging.

When I first started learning of ajrakh, a traditional form of block printing on cotton fabric, I wondered about the origin of my bedspread. Perhaps it wasn't Persian after all. Perhaps it was from the Indus Valley of Pakistan and India, the birthplace of ajrakh. Like ajrakh, the patterns on my piece are repetitive, and the colors—blues and reds—are similar. But traditional ajrakh patterns are rich with combinations of floral and geometric designs, and the only decorations on my piece are rows upon rows of horsemen.

I originally assumed that ajrakh artisans created the patterns directly, by dipping printing blocks in paint or dye and then pressing them onto the fabric. But as I delved deeper into my research, I discovered that the artisans achieve their results by working in reverse. They saturate the blocks either with a resist to prevent dye penetration or a mordant to fix the dye, and print those on the fabric. They then submerge the printed fabric in dye vats.

The outcome depends on the placement of the resist and the mordant, and also on the chemical reaction between a particular dye and the printed mordant. Each color on the finished piece requires a different combination of resists, mordants, and dyes.

The printing blocks that hold the patterns are works of art in their own right. Expert carvers use simple tools to carve detailed designs into teak wood: geometric patterns, flora and fauna, paisleys, and designs within designs.

Like carving the blocks, the making of ajrakh is men's work. The process includes scouring, mordant and resist printing, and multiple dips in indigo and madder dye vats. Methods vary mostly in the proportion of ingredients, the length of time spent at each station, and the ordering of the steps. The details change from craftsman to craftsman, based on availability of raw materials, the weather, and different traditions and personal preferences.

The actual printing is an exacting process and requires a steady hand. Placing the block carefully beside or on top of previously printed areas ensures the continuity and accuracy of the overall design. It also prevents different colors from overlapping, so that outlines and fillers are in their correct positions.

In order to guarantee clear lines, the artisans also have to be careful at every step of the dyeing process—while dipping in the dye vats or washing (to remove resist and excess dye), they have to avoid smearing the mordanted areas.

Particularly skilled artisans make reversible ajrakh. When printing both sides, not only do they have to worry about placing the blocks just right, but they also have to take shrinkage into consideration. They have to print the reverse side while the print on the first side is still damp so the cloth will dry evenly, without distorting the lines of the patterns.

    Photos courtesy of Carol Ventura

Photo courtesy of Carol Ventura

The people of the Sindh Province of Pakistan consider ajrakh to be a symbol of their culture. Even today, wandering around the marketplace in Karachi, the capital of Sindh, you'll see men wearing ajrakh-printed turbans and shoulder cloths, and women with block-printed shawls draped over their shoulders.

Nowadays, in order to earn a living wage, many ajrakh craftsmen have globalized their customer base by adding scarves, pillowcases, tablecloths, bedspreads, and wall hangings to their repertoire.

When I first decided to write about ajrakh, I was excited to learn more about the piece my brothers bought me. After I completed my research, I examined the bedspread more carefully than I had before, and came away a tad let down. The design was clearly printed directly onto the fabric, rather than in reverse (which would have been the ajrakh way), and not very carefully at that. Also, giving additional consideration to the pattern of the horsemen and their attire, I now suspect it was not made in the Indus Valley, but indeed in Persia.

I still love it, because my brothers gave it to me, and it will continue to adorn my walls wherever I go.

Resources

Bilgrami, Noorjehan. *Sindh Jo Ajrak: Cloth from the Banks of the River Indus*. 2nd ed. Bangkok: White Orchid Books, 2006.
Willoughby, Janet. *Ajrakh: Mordant Resist, Batik and Tie Dye*. DVD. Surviving Traditions. Hampton, UK: Ends of the Earth, 2000.

CHAPTER 6

Estonia

Handknit Mittens

Had I lived among Estonians who practiced the traditional way, I would have been a total disgrace. I would have been that one girl who had to unravel my knitting time and again, never getting it quite right.

I am a fairly versatile knitter. I've knit lace, entrelac, and Aran. I'm up for anything, except for knitting with more than one color at a time—no matter what I try, the tension is too tight in places, too loose in others. I could never have produced Estonian mittens that look semidecent, let alone beautiful. And I certainly couldn't have filled a dowry chest like all the other girls in my village.

Filling a dowry chest with beautiful handmade articles was a matter of pride. It was a family affair; mothers started the process even before their daughter was born. Girls started knitting and weaving items for their dowry at a young age. There was a saying, "A daughter one foot tall should have a present chest half a foot high." After a bride's engagement, friends and family helped out by adding their own work to the chest.

By her wedding day, an Estonian bride from a family of average financial means was expected to produce approximately one hundred handwoven belts and fifty pairs of handknit mittens, in addition to socks, stockings, and other handmade articles.

Mittens play a major role in everyday life in Estonia, and not just to keep away the chill during the frigid winters. Many Estonians associate mittens with averting the evil eye. Handknit mittens feature prominently in rituals such as christenings, weddings, and funerals. They continue to play a substantial part in a variety of marriage customs in some rural regions of Estonia, where many of the traditions are still a vibrant part of the culture.

In the past, when a young man showed interest in a girl, a member of his family visited her home bearing a bottle of liquor. If the girl or her family rejected his advances, they returned the bottle untouched. To signify acceptance, they returned the bottle empty, with a pair of mittens or socks tied around it. This was the first of many handknit items that tradition required a prospective bride to present to members of the groom's family.

Once engaged, the groom and his best man visited the bride to arrange the wedding, and after dinner they exchanged presents. The bride's gifts to the groom and his best man always included mittens, of course.

The wedding celebration, which lasted several days, was split into two parts: the first, at the bride's house, and the second, at the groom's. On the actual wedding day, the bride left her house to move into her new home. On entering the groom's house, the bride left a pair of mittens at every threshold.

The bride and groom consummated their marriage that night. The opening of the dowry chest took place the next day. Did the groom's family crowd around the bride as she pulled gift sets out of the chest? Or did they stand aside, seemingly aloof? Did the in-laws inspect every item for quality? Did they show their admiration or disdain, or did they keep their opinions to themselves?

Gift sets varied depending on the affluence of the bride's family. A complete set consisted of stockings, woven garters,

Photos courtesy of Kristi Jõeste

and mittens. A bride from a wealthy home produced a large gift set that included additional items, a scarf or a shirt, for example. A poor bride gave half a set—mittens or stockings. At several points during the merrymaking, the bride also presented gifts—a pair of mittens, stockings, or a belt— to those who helped perform the various rites.

Superstitions about Estonian handknit mittens were not limited to protection against the evil eye. In some districts, the groom wore mittens throughout the wedding day to ensure the birth of a son. Western Estonians believed that dreaming of white mittens was a portent of the death of a neighbor. Turning mittens and socks inside out was supposed to help lost travelers find their way. And when standing for trial, criminals wore mittens with a "whipping post" pattern in the hope of preventing corporal punishment.

Most Estonian mitten knitters of today knit two-color geometric patterns. Usually, the entire surface of the mitten is covered with repeats of motifs. If the design is relatively large, knitters will use repeats of a smaller, simpler version for the thumb. But many mittens bear a single motif or have a pattern around the cuff and nowhere else. The motifs, representing aspects of daily life, have names such as cat's paw, piglet, strawberry blossom, bean leaf, elk horn, saw blade, and whipping post.

After the introduction of aniline dyes, knitters on the island of Muhu in western Estonia created patterns with combinations of bold colors. In the rest of Estonia, the colors were more subdued. The pattern on the body of the mitten was either in a dark color, such as black or blue, on white back-ground, or white on a dark background, possibly with a touch of color—red, yellow, or green—on the cuff.

Cuffs on older mittens were very narrow and simple, several rows of ribbing or a braided cast-on. Toward the end of the nineteenth century, wider striped cuffs became popular. Today, knitters of Estonian mittens knit a broad variety of cuffs, including lacy zigzags, scalloped edging, entrelac, diamonds, fringes, some with stripes, and others with pattern repeats.

For years, I've ogled Fair Isle knit vests, handknit Icelandic sweaters, and Estonian mittens, but I couldn't justify the purchase—I was a knitter, after all. Finally, after years of resisting the temptation of purchasing Estonian mittens, researching this article tipped me over the edge—I now own a pair (pictured on page 42).

They are patterned with repeats of Xs and Os, charcoal on white, and the cuff has a slightly larger version of the same pattern, but the colors are reversed. And the tension is just right, throughout.

Resources

Bush, Nancy. *Folk Knitting in Estonia: A Garland of Symbolism, Tradition, and Technique*. Loveland, CO: Interweave, 1999.

Nargi, Lela. *Knitting around the World: A Multistranded History of a Time-Honored Tradition*. Minneapolis: Voyageur, 2011.

CHAPTER 7

China

Miao Pleated Skirts

I watch the procession, fascinated by the girls' festive regalia. Their tin headdresses and lavish jewelry sway and jingle with their every step. They're all chattering and laughing, probably excited to participate in the Chinese New Year's celebration.

But then I notice her, the one sulking, unhappy in her role. She's reluctant to dance; she barely jingles. I take a closer look. The tin becomes a minor distraction as her pleated skirt catches my full attention. I've never seen such fine pleating before—it must consist of hundreds, if not thousands, of pleats.

The Miao of Guizhou, China, place a high value on these elaborately embellished festival costumes, their main outlet for artistry and craftsmanship. The traditional dress among the Miao varies greatly from group to group. The locals nicknamed the groups based on

distinguishing characteristics of their dress: White Miao, Blue Miao, Flowery Miao, Long-Skirted Miao, and Short-Skirted Miao.

Though the styles of the traditional clothing differ from group to group, some features are common to all of them. For example, full festival wear among the Miao always includes a pleated, wraparound skirt.

Lengths range from miniskirts to ankle length. They can be made from hemp, ramie, or cotton, all fibers that are locally grown. Color and embellishment vary, as does the fineness of the pleats. The most common fabric colors are white, indigo, black, and green. Some skirts are monochromatic; others include decorative elements, such as embroidery, appliqué, or batik.

Pleating techniques also vary throughout the province. Some of the Miao pleat their skirts by smocking: they stitch several rows along the top few inches of the skirt, then draw the stitching tight to form the pleats. The smocking can be simple or patterned.

Others form the pleats through labor-intensive methods that take several days to complete. These pleating techniques are similar throughout the region, though some of the details differ slightly, depending on the group, the village, or the artisan.

In most cases, the artisan wraps a loosely gathered length of cloth around a bamboo cylinder or wooden barrel, secures the cloth to the cylinder with a rope, and dampens it with water or a starchy solution. She then makes the pleats by pinching the cloth with her fingers, pressing each new pleat against the previous ones, forming an accordion-like effect.

The pleating is particularly fine in southern Guizhou Province. I watched a video of a Miao woman pleating an indigo-dyed skirt. I was mesmerized by her nimble fingers dancing across the virgin fabric, leaving tiny, even pleats in their wake.

When the artisan finishes pleating the entire piece, she ties ropes firmly around the pleated cloth on the cylinder and leaves it to dry in the sun.

When it's dry, she removes the ropes and unwinds the fabric without disturbing the pleats. She bastes the fabric at the waist, running the needle through the peak of each pleat. She then stitches a waistband onto the pleated cloth, while keeping the pleats intact, and attaches a narrow strip of cloth to be used as a belt. Finally, she rolls up the finished skirt and winds a rope tightly around it.

Watching the unhappy girl in the procession, I wondered about keeping those pleats sharp. Did they repleat the skirts after each use? The answer surprised me in its simplicity: upon their return home from the festival, each girl or woman removes her skirt carefully, rolls it into a bundle, ties it up, and stores it until the next celebration—no ironing necessary. No washing either.

Resources

Corrigan, Gina. *Miao Textiles from China.* Seattle: University of Washington Press, 2001.

Torimaru, Sadae, and Tomoko Torimaru. *Imprints on Cloth: 18 Years of Research among the Miao People of Guizhou, China.* Translated by Yoshiko I. Wada and Nancy Salumbides. Fukuoka, Japan: Akishige Tada, 2004.

CHAPTER 8

Philippines

Piña Cloth

I stopped dead in my tracks when I caught sight of my colleague Tim in the hallway. He was wearing a translucent shirt that reached below the hips. I'd seen plenty of fine weaving before, but nothing as fine as the shirt he was wearing.

"What *is* that?" I exclaimed.

He touched the hem. "It's a barong. It's really comfortable. More than a jacket and tie. Roomy. Soft. It wears almost like a T-shirt."

It was November 2013, shortly after Typhoon Yolanda struck the Philippines, wreaking havoc throughout many of the islands. Tim was wearing one of his barongs while teaching his class to raise awareness for the victims of the typhoon.

Baro is the Tagalog word for "dress"; *barong* means "dress of," and *baro ng Tagalog* translates into "dress of the Tagalog people." Historically, the Tagalog people lived on the island of Luzon, which lies on the northern end of the Philippines. The baro ng Tagalog, or barong for short, is the formal men's wear of the Philippines. Filipino men wear the barong untucked with an undershirt, which nowadays is a white T-shirt.

The intricate embroidery down the front can be quite spectacular, but the barong's most striking feature is the fabric—lustrous, sheer piña cloth.

The barong of today evolved from the cotton baro that the Tagalog people wore during the pre-Hispanic era. In time, probably to cope with the heat and humidity of the tropical climate, the Tagalog replaced cotton with the lighter piña cloth.

In the wake of World War II, the barong evolved into a symbol of the Filipino national identity. Filipino men wore it proudly to formal ceremonies and important celebrations.

The creation of piña cloth from fiber to fabric is a labor-intensive process that lies within the women's domain. Piña artisans harvest the fibers from mature leaves of red Spanish pineapple. Many artisans still extract the fibers by hand, scraping off the top layer of the leaves with coconut husks or pieces of broken china to expose the coarser bastos fibers (which they set aside for the production of string). After stripping off the bastos fibers, the women repeat the process to reveal the finer liniwan fibers, which they earmark for weaving into piña cloth.

They knot single filaments together to produce single-filament yarns of workable length for the warp and weft. Though the artisans weave the fabric in a simple over-under plain weave, they cannot let their minds wander as they work. Because of the delicate nature and texture of the fine fibers, they have to constantly monitor the warp for breakage. Also, in order to create the airy fabric, they have to beat the weft down with a light hand.

Due to the time-consuming and exacting nature of the process, the number of piña weavers has been dwindling. As a result, piña barongs have become prohibitively expensive, and the vast majority of modern barong wearers now don shirts made of alternative sheer fabrics. Two options are the less expensive jusi—originally made from abaca (banana fibers), and, more and more, mass-produced silk (or a silk-polyester blend) from China.

Over the last two decades, the fashion industry has brought about a revival of the art of piña weaving. Designers no longer limit the use of piña cloth to the traditional baro ng Tagalog. There is increasing demand for piña wedding gowns, blouses, and other formal attire for women as well as men.

Piña cloth caught the attention of the international community through Oliver Tolentino, a Filipino designer now residing in the United States. Within weeks of opening his boutique in Beverly Hills, LA Fashion Week contacted him. TV host Maria

Menounos wore one of his piña creations to the 2012 Emmy Awards, and singer Carrie Underwood wore one to an *American Idol* performance in 2013.

Despite the demand, piña weavers continue to produce the cloth the traditional way, by hand. Tolentino, proud of his origins and a promoter of ecofriendly textiles, works directly with the weavers, discouraging them from mixing synthetic fibers, such as rayon or polyester, in the weave. However, to make the cloth more affordable, weavers do mix in natural fibers, including silk, cotton, or abaca.

When my colleague Tim and his Filipino wife, Fran, got married, they held wedding ceremonies both in the US and the Philippines. At their church wedding in the States, Tim wore a tuxedo. But for the ceremony in the Philippines, he chose to follow local custom and wore a barong. Not being a wealthy celebrity, he forewent a piña or piña blend barong and wore a finely woven silk one, instead.

Resources

Constante, Agnes. "Weaving Traditions Alive: Philippine Artists Featured in Int'l Market Seek to Spur Interest in Traditional Art." *Asian Journal MDWK Magazine*, July 9, 2015, http://asianjournal.com/aj-magazines/philippine-weaving-traditions-featured-in-12th-annual-international-folk-art-market/.

Eslit, Nila. "Fashion Acknowledges Pina Fabric: The Revival of an Old Industry." *Wall Street International*, May 25, 2015, http://wsimag.com/fashion/14855-fashion-acknowledges-pina-fabric.

Fitzgerald, Benjamin. "Piña Couture: Pineapple Fiber Makes Fabric in the Philippines." *Le Souk Magazine*, March 5, 2015, lesouk.co/articles/material-inspiration/pina-couture-pineapple-fiber-makes-fabric-in-the-philippines.

Flaherty, Fran. Filipino activist, private communication, 2013–2017.

Mariano, Chris. "Pina Weaving: Weaving Fabric from Pineapple Leaves." Coursera ADLS 2014—People, Places, Things: Piña Cloth (YouTube video), April 16, 2014, youtube.com/watch?v=dZ4iUdXPcZQ.

Moral, Cheche V. "Oliver Tolentino—How He Ended Up Dressing Carrie Underwood, Anna Paquin, Fergie, et al." Inquirer.net, May 10, 2013, http://lifestyle.inquirer.net/102599/oliver-tolentino-how-he-ended-up-dressing-carrie-underwood-anna-paquin-fergie-et-al/.

Rodell, Paul A. *Culture and Customs of the Philippines*. Westport, CT: Greenwood, 2001.

CHAPTER 9

India

Zari Brocade

My father traveled to India several times during my childhood. He always came back bearing exotic gifts. The one gift I remember vividly is the wedding sari he pulled out of his suitcase with reverence: a deep-maroon silk sari, embellished with gold brocade. I was awestruck by the sheen, the clingy softness, and how it rustled as Dad draped it over my arm. But I was most taken by the exquisite gold patterns along the border. It is still one of my most treasured ethnic textiles.

I recall Dad speaking of his visit to Banaras, a city in the state of Uttar Pradesh in northern India. After poring through various books and websites, I am convinced that my sari is a Banarasi sari.

Banaras, also known as Varanasi, is the last remaining Indian center of the zari (gold or silver thread) brocade-weaving industry. Brocade is a patterned weave that overlays the background cloth, similar in appearance to dense satin stitch embroidery. Traditional patterns include floral, paisley, trellis, or lattice designs, on the textile borders or covering the entire piece.

Originally, zari thread was made of genuine silver, often with a gold wash or plating. Zari makers recycled old zari saris whose silk fabric had become worn by melting down the damaged saris to silver ingots. They molded the silver into new zari thread by flattening it into narrow strips. Some artisans wove the brocade with the flattened silver wire, but most zari artisans wove with thread they formed by winding the flattened strips around silk or cotton threads. To create

golden thread, they plated the silver thread with gold.

During the Industrial Revolution, when the cost of gold and silver made traditional zari prohibitively expensive, electroplated copper wire replaced pure silver. Modern chemicals were (and are) used to impart a golden hue, replacing actual gold. When copper became too expensive, it was replaced by silver-burnished polyester thread, which is lighter weight and doesn't tarnish easily.

Unfortunately, advances in technology and subsequent mass production of cheap imitations diminished appreciation for the art and respect for the artisans. Earning a living as a zari weaver became next to impossible. Afraid that the tradition of zari brocade weaving would die out, several textile marketers and designers stepped in to combine tradition with modern tastes, to make the textiles more marketable.

Today, many zari weavers add modern designs to their repertoire of brocade patterns. Many also weave stoles and scarves, as well as saris—not only do they draw a

    Photo courtesy of Carol Ventura

broader customer base, but the smaller items are more cost effective than saris.

I love saris and personally prefer the traditional patterns to the dramatic geometric motifs that embellish a significant number of modern zari saris. But I'm also realistic about market pressures and the importance of protecting both the traditions and the livelihoods of these dedicated artisans.

Not long ago, I purchased a zari woven silk scarf for my mother. It's dark forest green, with a silver brocade strip along one of the borders. Though I didn't have the opportunity at the time to examine it closely, I suspect that the metallic-looking threads were silver-burnished polyester. Still, the depth of the color pulled me in, just as the deep maroon of my own sari does, and the rich silver brocade was exquisite.

Photos courtesy of Sahapedia: An Open Encyclopedia on Indian Culture and Heritage, sahapedia.org

Resources

Jaitly, Jaya. *Woven Textiles of Varanasi*. New
    Delhi: Niyogi Books, 2014.
Lynton, Linda. *The Sari: Styles, Patterns,
    History, Techniques*. New York: Thames
    & Hudson, 1995.

CHAPTER 10

India

Patan Patola

I can picture myself stretching a loom's width of warp threads along the side of a road, as they do in Guatemala with single ikat. I can see myself checking my pattern every time I finish wrapping a section of bundles of thread.

But my imagination fails me when I try to envision following the rest of the steps to create exquisite double-ikat textiles in the Patan tradition. I'm sufficiently familiar with the process of single-ikat weaving to appreciate the work that goes into the spectacular ikat textiles from Indonesia and Guatemala, and to be completely in awe of the stunning double-ikat work of the Patan weavers in the state of Gujarat, India.

In single-ikat weaving, artisans resist-dye the warp or the weft to form patterns in the weaving. They tightly wrap bundles of threads to form resist areas, so that when

they dip the threads in a dye vat, only the parts that aren't wrapped absorb the dye. In double ikat, or patola, the Patan weavers resist-dye both warp and weft threads. The designs emerge as the weft threads interlace with the warp, one row at a time.

Patan patola, or double ikat, from the city of Patan (in the state of Gujarat in western India), is an especially meticulous technique. There is no room for error. Patola spinners ply exactly eight silk filaments together to form the warp and weft threads, and in order to minimize unevenness in the coloring, patola artisans bleach the threads in preparation for tie dyeing.

Before the warp and weft wrapping can begin, Patan patola designers draw the ikat patterns on graph paper. The patterns vary depending on the customer base. Purely geometric and floral patterns cater to the Muslim community, and patterns involving dancing girls, elephants, and parrots appeal to the non-Muslims.

One artisan wraps the warp threads, and a second artisan wraps the weft. The artisan who wraps the warp threads follows the same steps as single (warp)–ikat weavers, stretching the warp across the room or courtyard. The weft wrapper stretches the weft in a zigzag back and forth across a frame of length equivalent to the width of the sari. Then, continually referencing the design, the two artisans tightly wrap corresponding bundles of thread with cotton yarn.

Once tied, it's time to dye the warp and weft. After dyeing the silk threads in one dye vat, patola dyers untie some of the wrappings, so that the color in the next vat penetrates the thread in the correct places. They repeat the sequence of wrapping, dyeing, and unwrapping for each color in the pattern.

Warping the loom comes next. The artisans place the dyed warp threads on the loom in sequence to ensure the continuity of the pattern. Unlike warp-ikat weavers, patola weavers also have to be careful winding the weft onto bobbins, keeping track of the correct order, to preserve the integrity of the design.

The weaving itself is, of course, also painstaking. The tension on the warp has to be uniform throughout, and the designs on the warp and weft have to line up perfectly. Usually, two weavers sit side by side at the loom, checking and double checking the emerging pattern, tweaking the weft thread a touch to the left or a tad to the right, flicking warp threads to make sure they don't shift sideways.

The Patan patola technique is so labor intensive that weaving a single sari takes four to six months. Currently, only three families of the Salvi caste in Patan still weave genuine patola. As a consequence, the Patan weavers have trouble meeting the demand for true patola saris. You will not find Patan patola saris in stores or showrooms—they all are special ordered, and there is a waiting period of several years.

It should come as no surprise that cheap imitations of the Patan patola are available. One such product is the patolu sari, which is a weft ikat in patterns mimicking the Patan patola designs. At the mass-market level, machines print patola-like designs on synthetic fabric.

Unfortunately, the market for the genuine article is in steady decline. In order to stay afloat while safeguarding their traditions, the Patan weavers have resorted to weaving items other than saris, such as tablecloths and handkerchiefs, that have a faster turnaround. Tablecloths are easier to sell because they appeal to a broader market, and there's more demand for handkerchiefs because they are more affordable than the larger items.

A textile collector friend visited Patan but found no genuine patola in stock; she was able to procure only small samples. Even the samples were extraordinary. I still have trouble grasping the time and effort that went into them, but no trouble at all understanding why a true Patan patola sari commands top price.

Resources

Edwards, Eiluned. *Textiles and Dress of Gujarat*. Ahmedabad, India: Mapin, 2011.

Lynton, Linda. *The Sari: Styles, Patterns, History, Techniques*. New York: Thames & Hudson, 1995.

CHAPTER 11

Bhutan

Backstrap Weaving

Rinzin gestured toward her mother, Leki. "She's a weaver to the king."

Leki smiled and nodded. She spoke no English.

Noble Bhutanese families often employed several skillful weavers to provide textiles for their extensive needs. The daughter of the first king of Bhutan had more than one hundred weavers in her service. Leki Wangmo was a weaver to the third king, Druk Gylapo Jigme Dorji Wangchuck, who ruled from 1929 to 1972. (*Druk Gylapo* is the title, meaning Dragon King.)

Although, in general, men are better educated than women and women have a heavier workload, in many ways men and women have equal standing in Bhutan. There are, in fact, safeguards in the Bhutanese constitution to guarantee gender equality. Men are in charge of everything pertaining to religion (Buddhism), and women are in charge of everyday matters, including weaving.

Weaving is an ancient art in the Himalayan Kingdom of Bhutan, also known as the Land of the Thunder Dragon. The art is central to the culture and is present in all aspects of life, religious and secular. In the past, the Bhutanese used textiles for gift giving and as a form of currency for commerce and taxation. Until recently, *all* Bhutanese household textiles and clothing, both for everyday use and special occasions, were handwoven.

Most Bhutanese citizens live in the countryside. Rural weavers typically weave to supplement their family's income, often earning more than husbands who hold regular jobs. Weavers who live in the cities tend to limit their weaving to items for their own households.

For the most part, weaving continues to pass from mother to daughter. (Embroidery and mending lie within the men's domain.) Rinzin Wangmo's grandmother, Dorgi, also a weaver of renown, taught Rinzin's mother, Leki, and Leki taught Rinzin.

Originally, Leki wove to support her family. But in the 1990s, as her reputation spread, she started teaching young villagers who wanted to hone their skill and young women who didn't have the opportunity to learn from their mothers. Once her students feel proficient as weavers, usually within

two years, they set off to earn a living through their craft.

I met Leki and Rinzin Wangmo in 2006 at a weavers' conference. Rinzin was demonstrating weaving on the Bhutanese version of a backstrap loom. I was fascinated—had I not seen her weaving the intricate inlay patterns with my own eyes, I would have assumed that they were embroidered.

I spent much of my time at the conference sitting in their booth, watching Rinzin manipulate the warp and supplementary weft to produce the beautiful effect. And we talked about weaving, their merchandise, and their lives in Bhutan.

Rinzin showed me the proper way to present textiles as gifts to the king: she folded several pieces carefully, piled them in a particular order, and then stood up straight and placed the pile on her shoulder. At the time, I didn't appreciate the details of her presentation. I didn't understand that there was a special etiquette for presenting gifts of textiles.

Bhutan has a long tradition of giving textiles as gifts to celebrate special occasions, including promotions and rites of passage such as weddings, births, and deaths. Traditional gifts of textiles consist of a package of a silk scarf plus three, five, seven, or nine new pieces of handwoven cloth; the status of the giver and receiver determines the exact number.

Nowadays, large fabric shops provide prearranged gift packages. In addition to the requisite silk scarf, these packages may include machine-made yardage to augment three handwoven pieces. Gift packages consisting of a silk scarf and, instead of textiles, an envelope containing money are becoming more common.

Rinzin explained that Leki learned the craft of dyeing as well as weaving from her mother, Dorgi, who was a dyer to the king. But finding natural dyeing too arduous, Leki prefers weaving. She was eight years old when she started weaving and, over the years, honed her skills and became a master weaver of Bhutan.

The weavers from south and central Bhutan use horizontal looms, with cotton and yak fiber for their yarn. Backstrap weaving is native to eastern Bhutan; backstrap weavers use silk and cotton, which is more conducive to the intricate patterns they are known for. Unlike many Bhutanese weavers, Leki and Rinzin weave both on a backstrap loom and a horizontal frame loom.

The backstrap loom that Rinzin used at the conference had two warp beams attached to a wooden frame. Normally, in Bhutan, she would have nailed the frame to a wall, but in the booth setting, Rinzin placed the frame in a stand to keep it upright on the convention hall floor.

One warp beam fits in slots near the top of the frame, and the other fits in slots at the bottom of the frame. The warp is circular, slanting upward from the breast beam, away from the weaver, around the upper warp beam, down and around the lower warp beam, and back to the breast beam.

Rinzin sat on the floor in front of the loom frame, and, like all backstrap weavers, she became an integral part of the loom—the tensioning device—by attaching herself to the breast beam via the backstrap. She positioned the strap around her back, just above her hips, and tied each end to the sides of the breast beam. Leaning against the backstrap while keeping her legs straight and bracing her

feet against the frame, she created an even tension on the warp.

Though backstrap weaving may seem like a primitive form of weaving, the patterns that backstrap weavers in many indigenous communities create can be extremely sophisticated. Bhutanese backstrap weavers are no different in this regard from their counterparts across the globe.

The plain-weave background on Rinzin's piece was warp faced (i.e., the warp was so dense that the weft was invisible), and the inlay patterns floated above it, as embroidery would. I watched closely as she wove. Her fingers flew as she raised and lowered individual warp threads to weave in the patterns, placing the colorful supplementary weft threads in complex designs.

I had no trouble following Rinzin's brocaded patterns; she wove under one warp thread, over ten, and under one, and then repeated her actions above each background row, back and forth, achieving a satin stitch-like effect. But I had to ask her to slow down when she demonstrated weaving the chain stitch-like patterns.

Embroiderers produce chain stitch by catching fabric with their needle and then looping the thread around the needle. Instead of catching small bits of fabric before forming the loop, Rinzin incorporated the chains into the weaving by forming loops around successive warp threads to achieve a similar effect.

After creating a chain length along the top of a row, she threw the shuttle to weave a new row of background plain weave and then continued creating her chains either directly upward, looping over the new row, or on a diagonal, looping over the row and one warp thread over. Once she brought the supplementary weft threads above the new plain row, she resumed the chain along its top.

She offered to let me try my hand at it, but I was afraid to ruin her beautiful work. Though the warp was narrow, each pattern row took her about ten minutes to complete. On average, it takes an accomplished weaver about three months to complete one length of patterned fabric. A kira, the traditional women's dress, requires three lengths. Not surprisingly, the number of Bhutanese weavers is on the decline; there are easier ways for young, educated women to earn a living.

Due to the relative isolation of Bhutan and limits set on the number of international visitors, weaving techniques and traditions remained practically unchanged for centuries. Even now, more than three decades since the Bhutanese government relaxed its visa restrictions, weaving traditions remain strong.

Until the 1980s, when tourism took root in Bhutan, few outsiders had heard of Bhutanese handwoven textiles. Now, these textiles, with their intricate brocaded patterns and discontinuous, supplementary-weft, embroidery-like designs, are highly prized worldwide.

Photo courtesy of Wendy Garrity, Textile Trails

Since my first meeting with Rinzin and
Leki, I have come to own several Bhutanese
textiles. At that first meeting in 2006, I
purchased a piece that Rinzin had woven in
the traditional colors, a white cotton background with dark-blue and red inlay designs.

My favorite piece is a royal hand towel
that Leki wove on a backstrap loom. When I
bought it, Rinzin mentioned that Leki had
intended to present it to the king. I couldn't
imagine wiping hands, royal or otherwise,
on such a striking silk textile.

I asked Rinzin why Leki didn't follow
through with her intention. Apparently,
needing to subsidize a trip to the US, Leki
brought it with her for sale. I am grateful
she did.

Resources

Altmann, Karin. *Fabric of Life—Textile Arts in
    Bhutan: Culture, Tradition and Transfor-
    mation.* Boston: Walter de Gruyter, 2015.
Elder, Gaye E. "Leki and Rinzin Wangmo:
    Weavers of Bhutan." *Shuttle Spindle &
    Dyepot* 150 (Spring 2007).
Garrity, Wendy. "Kushu Techniques of
    Bhutan." *WARP Newsletter* 19, no. 1
    (Spring 2012): 1, 11.
Myers, Diana K., and Susan S. Bean, eds. *From
    the Land of the Thunder Dragon: Textile
    Arts of Bhutan.* London: Serindia, 1994.
Wangmo, Leki, and Rinzin Wangmo, of Leki
    Textiles and Weaving Studio, private
    communication, 2006–2017.
Wangmo, Rinzin. "Fifth Generation Weaver
    in Bhutan Continues Textile Traditions."
    WARP Newsletter 22, no. 1 (Spring
    2015): 1, 10.

CHAPTER 12

Scotland

Kilt Hose

While watching episodes from the TV series *Outlander* (a show about a woman who traveled back in time from 1945 to 1743 Scotland), I found that my attention was split between the story and opportunities to catch a glimpse of what the Scotsmen wore above the hemline of their kilts.

It wasn't their underwear, or lack thereof, that I cared about—it was their stockings that piqued my curiosity. Were they woven or hand knitted? Did they match the tartan of their kilts? Were they patterned or plain?

Originally, Scotsmen wore dark-saffron, loose-fitting tunics and capes and went bare legged. Exposed to the elements, their legs took on a reddish-brown tan; hence the nickname "Redshanks." By the seventeenth century, they replaced the tunic with the plaid great kilt and, later still, with the kilt

as we know it today, a pleated, tartan wraparound skirt, the "little kilt."

The first leg coverings the Scots wore with kilts were leggings made of woven fabric, usually cut and sewn from the same fabric as their tartan kilt. The wearers bound the leggings at the knee with fringed garters, as they still do with the knitted hose of today.

The Highlanders continued to wear woven hose until the mid-1800s. Though knitting was already widespread in Scotland by the mid- to late 1700s, in the Highlands the craft became popular only during a famine in 1846–1848, when many women took up knitting to augment the family income.

To replace the woven tartan hose, Highland knitters developed a pattern similar in appearance to the tartans—they adapted standard argyle patterns, which

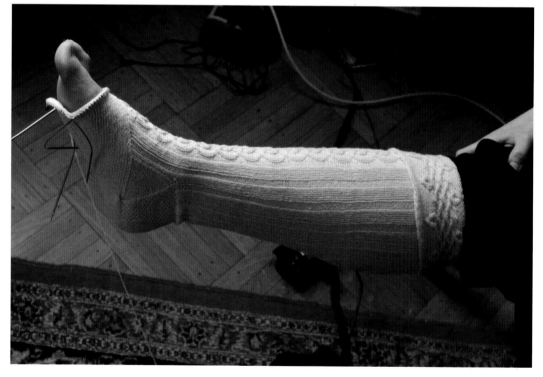

consist of repeats of diamond-shaped blocks of alternating colors with an overlay of diagonal lines that cross inside the solid diamonds. Highland argyle hose knitters often used more than the standard two colors for the diamonds.

Most sock patterns nowadays call for knitting in the round, with no seams. But because of the complexity of argyle patterns, hose knitters make them flat. When the knitting is completed, the knitters sew the flat pieces to form the stocking, taking care to match up the diamonds at the seam.

A simpler alternative to the argyle hose is the diced hose, which look like a checkered gingham or a simple two-color woven tartan, with no overlay. Diced hose have become more common than the argyle hose, because they're easier to knit and hence are less expensive. Many knitters simplified patterns further, creating single-colored handknit hose with knit-purl or cable patterns, making their hose more profitable. To make hand-knitted hose even more cost-effective, today's knitters often confine the patterns to the turned-down cuff.

Though the vast majority of kilt hose are now factory made, plenty of them are hand finished.

A Scottish friend of mine bought his one and only kilt to wear for his wedding celebration. He purchased the entire traditional ensemble, including kilt, jacket, sporran, and kilt hose. To my knowledge, he has worn it only twice. The first time was to the actual ceremony in Glasgow, and the second time was upon his return from Scotland, at a party to show it off to his American friends.

By the end of the night, quite inebriated, he demonstrated the freedom of movement his kilt afforded him by dancing on a table. I am sorry to report that his hose were factory made and had no patterning whatsoever, not even on the cuff.

I didn't check to see what he wore under the kilt itself.

Resources

Bush, Nancy. *Folk Socks: The History & Techniques of Handknitted Footwear*. Loveland, CO: Interweave, 2011.

Nargi, Lela. *Knitting around the World: A Multistranded History of a Time-Honored Tradition*. Minneapolis: Voyageur, 2011.

CHAPTER 13

Panama

Molas

I feast my eyes on the Kuna molas. Their colors and designs jump out at me; I don't know where to start. I want to see them all. I want to examine each one closely, which to me, like most textile artists, involves touching. I want to know every detail in the making of these molas—the patterns, the needlework, the stories, everything.

Among the Kuna, the word *mola* may allude to a cloud in the sky, a bird's feathers, skin, cloth, or clothing—it is a generic term for covering. The Kuna Indians of the San Blas Archipelago of Panama also use the term *mola* to refer to the colorful reverse appliqué front and back panels of the women's blouses, which is the meaning that we, of the industrialized parts of the world, associate with the word.

Appliqué is a form of embellishment that involves sewing pieces of fabric onto a background. Think of appliqué as working from the bottom up, starting with a ground fabric and adding layers to it. In reverse appliqué, the work is from the top down, starting by sewing together layers of cloth, then cutting shapes away from the top layer down to the ground fabric.

Kuna women use reverse appliqué to create figurative or geometric shapes outlined by colorful strips characteristic of molas. The seamstresses sew together layers of cotton fabric, each in a different color, and form the main shape by cutting larger shapes from the top layer, and progressively smaller shapes from successive underlayers, to produce the colorful outline.

The Kuna base their measure of a mola artist's skill on her creativity and design, color combinations, number of layers, and needlework. A mola panel can take one to six weeks to complete, since all the stitching is still done by hand. Kuna women experimented with machine sewing only briefly in the 1970s and discovered that it is easier to sew these intricate designs by hand.

To this day, the Kuna Indians have managed to hold themselves apart from the rest of the world, successfully preserving much of their culture and traditions.

According to Kuna legends, though molas came into being in primeval times, the knowledge of their making was hidden in Tuipis, one of the eight layers that make up the universe. Some scholars believe that the layers of fabric in the molas symbolize these layers of the Kuna universe.

Each layer of the universe is a world unto itself, each with a unique landscape. For example, one layer is mountainous, another is flat, and a third is a jungle or an ocean. Each layer is also associated with a particular aspect of the world we live in. Only some of the layers are accessible to the Kuna Indians, and those only by the shamans.

Tuipis, the fourth layer, is different. It is the origin of all things female, and no male shamans can enter it. One of the Kuna legends tells of a shaman's wife visiting Tuipis. Upon her return to this world, she brought the secrets of mola making to the Kuna women, including the designs.

According to the Kuna, mola motifs, whether contemporary or traditional, do not appear in dreams. The sources of inspiration for contemporary molas are the surrounding world or other molas, both new and old. Traditional patterns are those same designs on the molas that the shaman's wife brought back from Tuipis. These "grandmother molas," which include geometric and figurative motifs that symbolize creatures and scenery of Tuipis, have descriptive names, such as knee mola, heart mola, mountain shadow, rainbow, and turtle.

Many Kuna seamstresses supplement the main design with filler motifs, which consist of repeats of simple geometric shapes, usually done in regular appliqué. The Greek key pattern (square wave) is a common filler, as are chevrons, triangles, squares, and rectangles. Some fillers snake around the main motifs. Others are mazelike, possibly symbolizing the coral reefs or the paths between Kuna village huts.

There's a practical reason for stitching the fillers onto the ground fabric: it prevents the layers of the molas from coming apart or losing shape. But anthropologists theorize that the density of the fillers is related to the Kuna lifestyle, perhaps symbolic of the dense layout of the huts in the villages. Another theory is that fillers represent the verbal patterns heard in the chanting of the Kuna oral traditions—chanters are not allowed silent pauses. Or perhaps it is the other way around; the fillers in speech, housing, and mola designs are emblematic

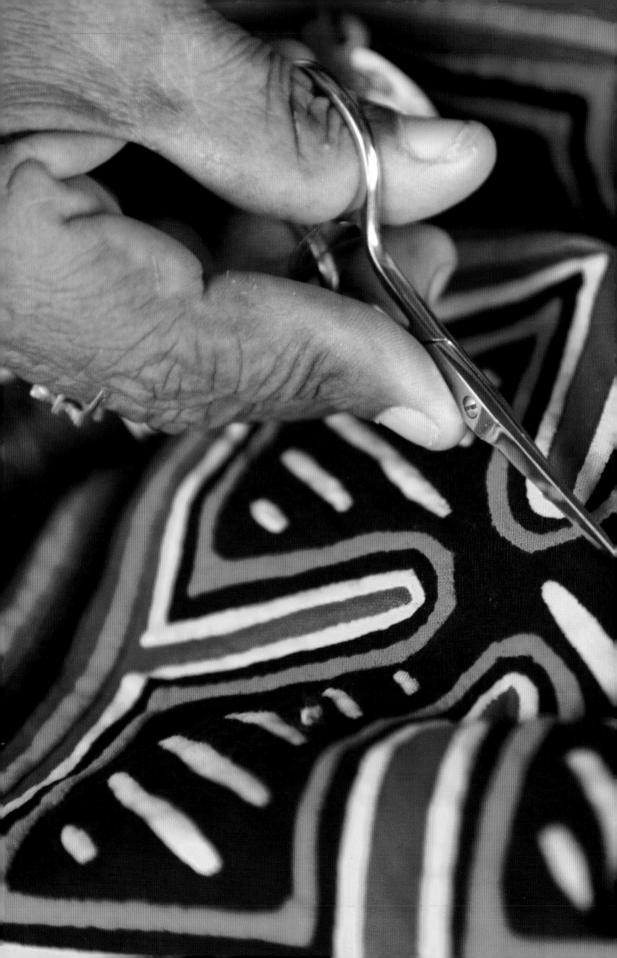

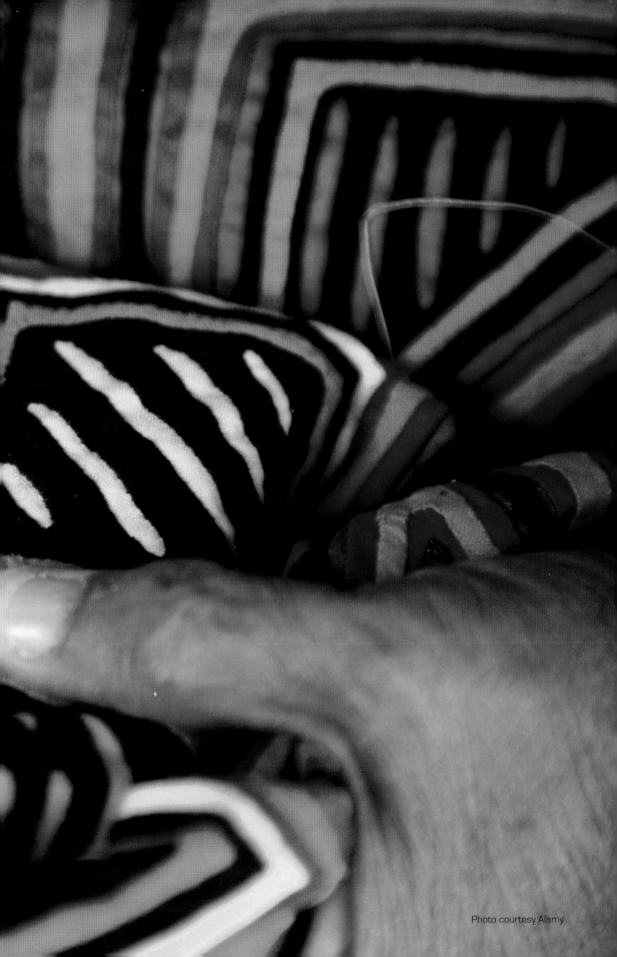

of some other cultural aspect of the Kuna Indians that outsiders have yet to identify.

Unfortunately, there is limited firsthand knowledge about Kuna mythology in general, and mythology associated with molas in particular, which makes it difficult to reconstruct the history of the technique. The Kuna shamans are reluctant to share information about the oral traditions, and there are no written accounts of their beliefs. In addition, creating molas is predominantly women's work, and Kuna women have very little direct contact with outsiders.

Though information about the making of molas is incomplete, historians and anthropologists agree that contrary to Kuna folklore, molas came into existence much more recently than primeval times.

The earliest eyewitness account is from 1681, when Scottish surgeon Lionel Wafer wrote about the Kuna lifestyle. He reported that the women wore simple cotton skirts and were naked from the waist up. He also mentioned the women's artistic prowess in body painting. He was particularly taken by the colorful figurative designs, "Birds, Beasts, Men, Trees, or the like," that decorated their nude torsos. Scholars believe that these body paint designs probably formed the foundation for mola motifs.

Various eyewitness reports since Wafer's time indicate that molas appeared no earlier than the second half of the nineteenth century, when the Kuna became less isolated after migrating to the islands from the Darien Jungle of Panama. Another piece of evidence that dispels the Kuna claims about the advent of mola making is that its precision requires materials and tools that come from the outside world:

mass-produced cotton fabric and thread, and steel scissors and needles.

There is some resentment among the Kuna over such allegations. By incorporating the art of creating molas into their core beliefs, they have asserted sole ownership over these breathtaking works of art. They feel that scholars from the developed world who challenge their beliefs disrespect their culture and minimize their accomplishments.

It's possible—probable, even—that at least some of the discrepancies between Kuna oral tradition and Western scholars' theories are rooted in the ambiguity of the word *mola* itself. Ancient Kuna may have used mola to refer to body paint. As new materials and tools became available, the meaning shifted and evolved until it became the word for the beautiful textiles we see today.

Resources

Gianturco, Paola, and Toby Tuttle. *In Her Hands: Craftswomen Changing the World*. New York: Monacelli, 2000.

Gillow, John, and Bryan Sentance. *World Textiles: A Visual Guide to Traditional Techniques*. New York: Thames & Hudson, 1999.

Perrin, Michel. *Magnificent Molas: The Art of the Kuna Indian*. Paris: Flammarion, 2000.

Puls, Herta. *Textiles of the Kuna Indians of Panama*. London: Shire, 1988.

CHAPTER 14

Thailand

Hmong Paj Ntaub (Story Cloth)

An enemy tank rolls over a tree, flattening it. Soldiers set village houses on fire. An airplane drops bags of rice. Soldiers beat Hmong men and boys to death. Lines of refugees wait to cross the Mekong River on inner tubes. Hmong women register at a refugee camp, rows and rows of plain buildings—the barracks—crowding the dusty field.

I have a hard time imagining the plump, smiling woman in the photograph in Linda Gerdner's *Hmong Story Cloths* as part of such violent and desperate settings. Yet, for several years, that was the life Manichan Xiong knew, and the life she re-created on cloth.

During the Vietnam War, many of the Laotian Hmong were strong supporters of the United States. Manichan's family helped rescue an injured American pilot. In retaliation, North Vietnamese soldiers killed her grandfather while she and her mother hid under the bed. Seeking revenge, Manichan joined the "Secret Army," an army of Laotian Hmong recruited by the CIA and trained to fight against the North Vietnamese.

After the US withdrawal from Laos in 1975, she, like many other Hmong US supporters, fled Laos with her family. In 1976, they arrived at the Ban Vinai refugee camp in Thailand, where they lived until she and her family were allowed entrance to United States five years later.

In the photo, Manichan Xiong's smile speaks of her pride in her creation, the wall hanging in the background. It's a paj ntaub, also called story or flower cloth, a beautiful piece of colorful embroidery that tells her story and the story of her people, from their migration from China to Laos, to their escape into Thailand, to their lives in the refugee camps.

The Hmong, with no written language of their own, have a rich oral tradition, which has helped maintain their cultural identity through a turbulent history that threatened their very existence. Even after missionaries developed a written language for the Hmong in the early 1950s with some degree of success, Hmong elders continued to preserve their heritage by passing it on orally through the generations.

In the refugee camps, story cloths became a way to document and retain Hmong history and traditions. They were also an artistic outlet for the women—a way to show off their exquisite needlework, a source of pride among the Hmong. In addition, story cloths provided a much-needed source of income.

Men drew the outlines of the images on a background fabric, usually a blue cotton-polyester blend. Women then embroidered the images. And once the embroidery was completed, the needleworkers finished the cloth by framing it with a pieced-fabric border, often including a series of triangles to symbolize the highlands of Laos.

Embroiderers had no qualms about copying scenes from each other. They expressed their creativity through their skill with the needle, the intricacy of the details, and the way in which they altered the overall scene.

Some story cloths are pictorial representations of the Hmong experience during the Vietnam War and their flight across the Mekong River into Thailand. Others depict images from folktales and stories that help sustain oral traditions for future generations. And many, like the story cloth I own, portray the traditional lifestyle in the mountains of Laos.

Accounts about the origins of story cloths contain some discrepancies, possibly due to language issues; details may have been lost in the translation. Scholars agree that story cloths originated in the camps in Thailand, although it's not clear exactly how the idea came to life.

Manichan arrived with her family at the Ban Vinai Refugee Camp in Thailand in 1975. She spoke of a Thai man named David who suggested needleworking projects to the women and helped them build a shelter where they could gather and sew items for sale. Some refugees sold their embroidery directly to foreigners visiting the camps. Others sold their pieces through intermediaries to Hmong communities abroad, who, in turn, sold them in a broader market, often at craft fairs and other textile-related venues.

According to Manichan, in 1978 she thought of embroidering images that represented stories of Hmong history. Her first story cloth became a family affair—her nephew drew the outline of the figures in her vision on fabric, and Manichan and her sister embroidered the drawing.

It's not clear from the translation of Manichan's account whether she claimed to be the first to think of depicting various Hmong stories through her embroidery, the first to create a story cloth, or the first to represent the history of the Hmong.

However and whenever story cloths came into being, the technique that Hmong embroiderers use is common to most, if not all, story cloths. They start out with long satin stitch to fill in the drawn images and then outline the images with shorter satin stitch. Next, they add detail work, such as leaves on trees, facial features, and halters on beasts of burden.

In an effort to appeal to tastes of the developed world and increase marketability, story cloths continue to evolve. New themes are emerging. Religious motifs are increasing in popularity. Also, although traditional Hmong needlework is done in bright colors, the prevalent colors now are more muted and coordinated.

At first, the Hmong women continued to practice their needlework skills and make story cloths in their new home countries. But in their struggle to settle into their new lives, more and more women abandoned the art. Elders of the Hmong refugee communities fear that traditional needlework skills are in danger of extinction.

My story cloth represents the Hmong rural life before the Vietnam War. I bought it partly because I appreciated the work, but also because, as an ethnic-textile enthusiast, I feel an obligation to help perpetuate textile traditions by supporting Hmong textile artisans and by promoting their work.

Resources

Gerdner, Linda A. *Hmong Story Cloths: Preserving History & Cultural Treasures.* Atglen, PA: Schiffer, 2015.

Hickner-Johnson, Corey. "Taking Care in the Digital Realm: Hmong Story Cloths and the Poverty of Interpretation on HmongEmbroidery.org." *Journal of International Women's Studies* 17, no. 4 (July 2016): 31–48.

CHAPTER 15

Zimbabwe

Sadza Batik

Recipe for Sadza

1. Soak 2 cups of mealie-meal (cornmeal) in 4 cups of water in a saucepan for a couple of hours.

2. Stir the soaked cornmeal with a mugoti (wooden spoon), gradually adding water, to form a thick paste.

3. Boil 6 cups of water.

4. Place saucepan with the cornmeal paste on medium-high heat and gradually add boiling water while stirring vigorously with the wooden spoon to prevent lumps.

5. Bring to a boil.

6. Reduce the heat and continue cooking for about 5 more minutes while stirring, until it reaches the consistency of mashed potatoes.

Sadza, a thick cornmeal paste cooked in water, is a staple of the Shona diet. Instead of wasting the leftovers, the Shona either feed them to their goats or use them as a resist in their batiks.

Batik is an ancient textile technique in which artists apply a resist in a pattern to a piece of fabric before dyeing or painting it. The resist prevents the dye from penetrating the cloth. After drying the now-colored fabric, the artist removes the resist, so the fabric has a pattern in the predyed color of the fabric.

The Shona tribe of Zimbabwe is the largest indigenous group of the Bantu-speaking people in Zimbabwe. They're known for their rich cultural heritage, as well as their music, ironwork, pottery, and, most of all, their stone sculptures. (The word *Zimbabwe* is derived from a Shona word that means "house of stone.") Not as well known, but no less impressive, are their striking sadza batiks.

The art of batik is traditional to many indigenous groups across the globe. Archaeologists have discovered samples of batik on wrappings of Egyptian mummies from the fourth century BCE, and on textiles in central Asia and India from over 2,000 years ago. Scholars believe that batik originated in Asia and spread from there.

Asian batik artists usually use a hot-wax resist. African artists tend to use a variety of resists in their batik work, depending on the materials available to them. The Asante use primarily hot wax, the Yoruba use cassava starch or rice flour, the

Banama use mud, and the Shona use sadza, the cornmeal-based resist.

Shona batik artists, primarily women, outline shapes with the sadza resist. They then paint the textile—usually cotton, sometimes silk—with vibrant colors, painting the inside of the shape with one color and the outside with another. The resist forms a boundary to separate the two regions and prevents the two colors from bleeding into each other.

Sadza batik usually depicts folktales and stories from daily life in the village, such as clothed stick figures portraying dancers, warriors, and women at work. Pictures of shields with crossed spears appear on many sadza textiles, as do stylized images of animals; for example, elephants, crocodiles, fish, lizards, and birds.

Shona batik also contains geometric designs that range from the purely decorative to representations of traditional and mythical elements of Shona culture. The herringbone pattern represents the king as the backbone of society. Checkerboards are symbols of the interdependence between tribe members, such as marriage. Spirals symbolize the cosmic force, spiritual journeys, and the cycles of time and nature.

Traditional Shona batik artists usually work their designs in separate rectangular blocks within a complete panel. Some of the blocks contain repeats of spirals, parallel lines, zigzags, and other geometric motifs. Other blocks center on a single stylized image, usually with a frame of geometric repeats.

Photo courtesy of Sinja Streuper, Textura

Originally, like many other traditional African textiles, the prevalent colors in sadza cloths were earth tones. Now that textile inks are more readily available, the color-loving Shona use a much-broader palette.

The tradition of sadza batik is still very much alive today. The Shona continue to use the batiks to adorn traditional dress, mostly as a mark of prestige and seniority, as they did in the past, though now they usually limit wearing traditional attire to special occasions. They also use their textiles to create contemporary clothing for the global market. But the majority of sadza batik targets the tourist industry, in the form of wall hangings, tablecloths, and pillow covers.

Iva Penner, the woman who taught me the art of Shona batik, was a resident of Zimbabwe for several years. There she learned the art and has been practicing it ever since. She prepares the resist for her workshops by modifying the traditional sadza recipe, reprinted here with her permission.

Modification for Batik:

1. Add ½ tablespoon of salt as a preservative.
2. Place a small amount of water in a blender.
3. Blend while gradually adding sadza, until smooth.

Resources

Crowley, Daniel J. "African Crafts as Communication." *African Arts* 14, no. 2 (February 1981): 66–71.

Editors of Encyclopædia Britannica. "Shona People." In *Encyclopædia Britannica*. Last modified June 8, 2009, britannica .com/topic/Shona.

Kerlogue, Fiona. *Batik: Design, Style, and History*. New York: Thames & Hudson, 2004.

Penner, Iva. Artist, private communication, 2016.

Shepard, Lisa. *Global Expressions: Decorating with Fabrics from around the World*. Iola, WI: Kraus, 2001.

Tucker, Sarah. *Batik*. Marlborough, UK: Crowood, 1999.

CHAPTER 16

Ghana

Kente Cloth

"Once, long ago, in the Ashanti village of Bonwire in the country of Ghana, there lived two expert weavers. One weaver was called Nana Koragu. The other was Nana Ameyaw . . ."

So begins the Ghanaian legend of the birth of kente weaving, as told by Margaret Musgrove and Bat Favitsou Boulandi in *The Spider Weaver: A Legend of Kente Cloth*. The two weavers went into the forest to hunt, and on the way home they discovered a spider web "of wondrous design," such as they'd never seen before, which inspired them to create what became a new textile tradition. According to Musgrove and Boulandi, "At first they wove them in black and white thread, but in time they dyed their threads in bright colors and developed many new designs based on what she [the spider] taught them . . ." Today, we refer to cloth with the colorful designs as kente cloth.

In order to fully appreciate kente cloth, you have to give it a second look. Once you do, you'll want to give it a third look and a fourth.

Until I attended a presentation by Caphuchi Ahiagble, a master weaver from Ghana, I'd noted kente cloth only in passing, dismissing it as a patchwork of brightly colored, almost gaudy African textiles. Taking that second look, I came to appreciate it and give it that third and fourth look. Kente cloth is not, in fact, a patchwork cloth at all.

Usually, a piece of cloth is either all warp-faced weave (where the weft is practically invisible), all weft-faced (where the weft covers the warp), or balanced (both warp and weft are visible). Kente cloth combines both warp-faced and weft-faced weaves in a single piece.

Kente weavers weave the cloth in long, continuous, narrow strips (hence the term "strip weaving"). In the same strip, they alternate blocks of warp-faced weave (yielding vertical stripes) with blocks of weft-faced weave (yielding horizontal stripes). The artisans cut these strips of cloth off the loom and sew them together selvedge to selvedge to form cloth with a checkered appearance.

Most strip weavers in West Africa weave on narrow-band horizontal looms with one set of double heddles. Kente weavers use two pairs of harnesses, one to raise and lower every other warp thread, and the other pair to raise and lower alternating groups of six warp threads.

To produce the warp-faced blocks, the warp is dense enough to cover the weft when weaving under and over single warp threads, using the first set of harnesses. To weave the weft-faced blocks, kente weavers use the second pair of harnesses to weave over and under groups of six warp threads, covering the warp with the weft.

Strip weaving is exclusively a male occupation. Men and boys tend to everything associated with the weaving: winding thread on the bobbins, measuring the warp, warping the loom, and weaving. The weavers sit at carpenter frame looms, feet capering on the treadles to raise and lower the harnesses. Their hands dip, twist, turn, and glide like the spider in the legend, as they throw the shuttle back and forth and pick up threads to weave in inlay patterns with discontinuous supplementary warp.

Having observed many a weaver, both indigenous and nonindigenous, and being a weaver myself, I have seen many techniques and loom setups. The deceptively simple appearance of the wooden frame looms did not surprise me, nor did the speed at which the weavers worked, even the young boys.

Two things did strike me about kente weaving. One was the weavers' method of manipulating the harnesses. All treadle looms I'd seen, including my own, have treadles that we press down on and release to raise and lower threads to create an opening for the shuttle to perform its over-and-under dance. In kente weaving, the weavers tie one pair of harnesses (for weft-faced weaving) to a pair of pedals, which they press and release by using their heels. They tie the other pair to discs of calabash (or nowadays, often rubber), to manipulate the harnesses in the warp-faced blocks. They place the discs between their toes, like a flip-flop sandal, pulling and releasing to raise and lower the corresponding harnesses. So, for the weft-faced blocks, they work their heels, and for the warp-faced blocks, they work their toes.

The other thing that surprised me was their method of creating tension on the warp. The warping process includes tying the virgin warp to a heavy stone ledge, coiling up the remaining warp threads in the shape of a doughnut (Bobbo, Caphuchi Ahiagble's father, referred to it as a "crown" in his book), and then placing it on the ledge. The warp stretches across the

courtyard, from the loom out to the ledge. As the weaver advances the warp, winding the woven part onto the front beam, the warp pulls the ledge forward, the ledge's weight keeping the warp threads taut. When the ledge reaches close to the loom, it's time to untie the warp from the ledge, unravel the doughnut, move the ledge back across the courtyard, and retie the warp to it.

Many of us in the developed world associate kente cloth with the Asante, who form the majority of the population of West Africa. But, in fact, there are two kente traditions in Ghana: the better-known Asante kente, and the adanudo cloth of the Ewe tribe (also known as Ewe kente). Both tribes use the same equipment and techniques to produce cloth with a checkerboard appearance.

Even though they may look similar, there are some significant differences between the two kente styles. The Asante usually use silk to weave kente cloth, and the Ewe weavers weave mostly with cotton, though rayon is not an uncommon choice nowadays for both styles of kente cloth.

Both the Ewe and the Asante use pick-up to weave supplementary weft inlay into some of the warp-faced sections. All the Asante inlay patterns are geometric in nature. The Ewe patterns range from the pictorial motifs to the abstract, from zigzag and stars to representations of animals and objects from everyday life.

The colors in the two kente traditions are strikingly different. The Asante kente

combines bright colors—reds, yellows, greens, and blues—as well as black. Originally, the Ewe limited their colors to indigo and white. Now, they use a broader range of colors than the Asante, though the Ewe colors are more muted.

There are also more-subtle differences: unlike Asante weavers, the Ewe sometimes ply together two colors of the weft thread before weaving to create a speckled effect. Also, using a supplementary warp technique, some Ewe weavers form stripes of unwoven thread on the surface of the weaving.

Kente cloth is often referred to as "talking cloth." Unlike many other traditional textiles across the globe, where single motifs have meaning, in kente cloth the overall patterns have a significance as well, conveying a wealth of information including history, legends, proverbs, and messages.

Caphuchi brought several samples of Ewe kente with him to the presentation I attended, including a piece that conveyed the message "The problem is solved." Another, for a prospective son-in-law to present during marriage negotiations, meant "The ball is in your court." On the cover of his book *Master Weaver from Ghana*, the pattern of the cloth Bobbo Ahiagble is wearing is called *sedavor*, which translates to "Fences make good friends."

According to the Ghanaian legend, everyone in Bonwire wanted to wear this new cloth, but the king of the Asante decreed that only he could don it.

In time, kente attire was no longer restricted to the Asantehene (the king of the Asante), but he had exclusive access to a number of the patterns. Some of the king's more complex patterns required the use of a third pair of harnesses.

Unlike the Asante, the Ewe, with no history of a strong centralized form of government, made kente cloth available to anyone who could afford it.

Now, kente cloth is available for everyone to wear, whether Ewe or Asante. Perhaps a weaver presented the Asantehene with a cloth patterned with the message "One man cannot rule a country," and he took it to heart.

Photos courtesy of Carol Ventura

Resources

Ahiagble, Chapuchi. Ewe master weaver from Ghana, private communication, 2007.

Ahiagble, Gilbert "Bobbo," and Louise Meyer. *Master Weaver from Ghana*. Greensboro, NC: Open Hand, 1998.

Gillow, John. *African Textiles: Color and Creativity Across the Continent*. New York: Thames & Hudson, 2009.

Gillow, John, and Bryan Sentance. *World Textiles: A Visual Guide to Traditional Techniques*. New York: Thames & Hudson, 1999.

Hecht, Ann. *The Art of the Loom: Weaving, Spinning, & Dyeing across the World*. Seattle: University of Washington Press, 1989.

Musgrove, Margaret. *The Spider Weaver: A Legend of Kente Cloth*. Illustrated by Bat Favitsou Boulandi. Baltimore: Apprentice House, 2015.

Spring, Chris, and Julie Hudson. *Silk in Africa*. Seattle: University of Washington Press, 2002.

Willoughby, Janet. *Kente: Woven Ceremonial Cloths of Ghana*. DVD. Hampton, UK: Ends of the Earth, 2005.

CHAPTER 17

Ghana

Adinkra Cloth

The breeze carries the sound of music in through the open window of the rickety jeep. You crane your neck, searching for the source of the lively drumming accompanying voices raised in song. It comes in sight as your driver rounds the corner: men, women, and children in black clothing, some sitting in the shade of red and black canopies, others wandering around, and a few dancing to the beat of the drums. The men are clad in toga-like garments. The women wear three-piece outfits: a long wrap skirt; a drape that covers one shoulder, the breasts, and midriff; and a head tie.

In some cultures, funerals are somber affairs. In others, they're celebrations of life or a combination of the two. Colors signifying death vary as well, ranging from black, white, and gray to green, purple, and yellow.

The traditional fabric of Asante funeral garb is black adinkra cloth—block-printed repeats of geometric motifs covering the entire surface of black cloth. The contrast between the deep black of the background fabric and the luminous black sheen of the print is stunning.

Originally, the Asante wore adinkra garments only to signify mourning; now they wear adinkra to various special events in a variety of colors. White adinkra is the most common color for less somber affairs, but brown, tan, and gold cloth are also popular. Though funeral attendees still wear black adinkra, these days, close relatives wear red, or combinations of red and black.

Modern adinkra artisans use synthetic dyes in a broad range of colors to dye the background fabric, except when it comes to the black funeral cloth. For that, they continue to use the traditional dyeing techniques. The traditional black dye for the background cloth is made from the roots of the kuntunki tree. Master dyers dye and over-dye the fabric several times to achieve a sufficient depth of color.

Since customary Asante clothing requires large swaths of fabric, tailors join lengths of dyed adinkra cloth together. In most cases, the tailors just machine-sew the joins. In the past, cloth with elaborate joins was available only to royalty, but nowadays, anyone with the means can purchase and wear adinkra cloth with colorful trim. The more affluent adinkra wearers commission ornate joins, where artisans either attach the lengths of fabric with dense faggoting stitch or feather stitch in bright-colored thread, or sew a strip of colorful kente cloth between the two pieces.

Carvers hand-carve the stamps for block printing from thick-skinned calabash gourds. Each motif holds meaning; some symbolize proverbs, sayings, or human values, and others stand for historical events. The symbol for "God never dies; therefore I cannot die" represents life after death, "wind-resistant house" indicates fortitude, "ram's horn" means concealment, "bite not one another" signifies unity and avoiding conflict, and "moon and star" implies faithfulness.

The printers use a gleaming black pigment that they make from the bark of the badie tree. After soaking pieces of bark in water, they pound it to a pulp and then boil the pulp in water. After straining the mixture, they distill the remaining liquid until it reaches a tar-like consistency, called adinkra medicine.

Some adinkra printers divide the fabric into sections. They first print a grid, either with single straight lines, parallel lines (with a comb), or repeated motifs. Next, they work within each section, stamping either a lone motif or repeats of it, depending on the size of the section. However, most adinkra cloth designs don't include grids; instead, each length of fabric bears repeats of a single motif.

Traditionally produced adinkra is expensive. To reduce the cost, many Asante of lesser means recycle worn funeral attire

that has lost its luster by over-dyeing the cloth and refreshing the printed motifs, rather than buying a new cloth.

Today, some adinkra artisans use screen-printing methods with water-based fabric paint rather than the traditional block-printing techniques. They draw adaptations from traditional stamps, by hand or on a computer, then transfer the images onto screens.

Wandering around in the market town of Kumasi, which lies within the adinkra center of Ghana, you will see booths with adinkra cloth in a myriad of colors; some in piles, others hanging, flapping in the breeze. The temptation to purchase a piece on the spot will be hard to resist. However, given the choice, before shopping in Kumasi, I'd make a trip to the center of adinkra printing, the nearby village of Ntonso, to see the artisans at work, up close and personal, and to try my hand at adinkra printing.

Resources

Gillow, John. *Printed and Dyed Textiles from Africa*. Fabric Folios. Seattle: University of Washington Press, 2001.

Gillow, John. *African Textiles: Color and Creativity across the Continent*. New York: Thames & Hudson, 2016.

Gillow, John, and Bryan Sentance. *World Textiles: A Visual Guide to Traditional Textiles*. New York: Thames & Hudson, 1999.

Ventura, Carol. "The Twenty-First Century Voices of the Ashanti Adinkra and Kente Cloths of Ghana." Paper presented at the 13th Biennial Symposium of the Textile Society of America, titled *Textiles and Politics*, held 19–22 September 2012 in Washington, DC.

Willoughby, Janet. *Adinkra: Printed Ceremonial Cloths of Ghana*. DVD. Hampton, UK: Ends of the Earth, 2005.

CHAPTER 18

Haiti

Vodou Flags

You're not sure where to start—the images are dazzling and they all call your name. A myriad of colorful vodou flags, heavy with beads and sequins, cover the walls of the gallery. Dancing with reflections of light, they cry for attention, first one and then the next and the next. Though itching to purchase one, you decide to wait until after you visit the nearby vodou temple. You want an authentic vodou flag, one that carries a traditional story. Apparently, that congregation owns six flags, and before you return to the gallery to buy one, you want to learn about the meaning behind them—you want to hear more about the vodou religion.

The entertainment industry has led many of us to associate the word *vodou* (or voodoo) with zombies, dolls bristling with pins, and black magic. In reality, vodou is a bona fide religion, the primary religion in Haiti. It is a blend of the West African

Yoruba religion, tenets of the indigenous people of the Caribbean, and Roman Catholicism, reflecting the Haitian ethnic and cultural diversity.

According to vodou theology, various deities govern the spiritual and worldly realms. Each deity is either cool and soothing or hot and harsh, or forms a bridge between the two, thus providing a balance. Some of them rule natural phenomena; others are responsible for human struggles and achievements. Several are in charge of health, death and birth, and wealth. The deities also act as intermediaries between humans and Bondye, a higher power who is completely removed from the functioning of the universe.

The deities possess individual members of the congregation and speak through them to address the assembly and provide guidance in both the spiritual and practical

congregations possess additional flags, usually up to a total of six. These represent the six most important deities: Ogou and Danbala, plus Ezili Freda, the goddess of love; the Gede siblings, who are the guardians of the realms of the dead; Loko, the guardian of the temple; and Ayizan, a mother figure and healer who watches over the priestesses and directs the instruction of new initiates.

Traditional vodou flags depict representations of the deities in the form of ritualistic emblems, Catholic saints, or other figurative images. Ezili Freda's symbols are hearts and the Virgin Mary. Saint Isidore the Farmer stands for Azaka, the god of agriculture. Mermaids represent La Sirène, queen of the ocean and patroness of music.

The custom of using ceremonial flags as an essential part of religious rituals originated in Africa. Enslaved people from Africa brought the tradition to Haiti during the colonial era, helping them maintain their cultural identities through centuries of dehumanizing conditions.

Like many traditions, flag styles changed over time. They became more elaborate, and the variety in the design of the motifs increased. In the nineteenth century, most flag makers embroidered images on simple blue, red, or white banners. Modern flag makers embellish flags by sewing on a dense coating of beads and sequins, producing sometimes ostentatious works of art.

Each flag contains a central motif, a background, and a border. The background

aspects of the worshipers' lives. Priests invoke the spirits through prayer, sacrifice, ritual music, dance, and flag processions.

Due to the labor-intensive and artistic nature of flag making, the flags are pricey. Despite the cost, most vodou societies own at least two. According to some priests, only two flags must be present during ceremonies: one that represents Ogou the warrior, and one that signifies Danbala, who together with his wife, Ayida, is responsible for birth and creation. Extremely wealthy

Photos courtesy of Laurie Beasley, Ridge Art

frames the central motif. In older flags, the sequins and beads in the background were sparse, adding glitter to the fabric without covering it. Nowadays, the background, like the central motifs, is lush with sequins and beads. Usually, as in earlier flags, the background consists of a single color, though some artists divide the field into simple geometric shapes of different colors. Border patterns, originally almost nonexistent, have become more prominent and ornate.

Experts measure the quality of modern flags by the tightness of sequin and bead arrangement, the evenness of the pattern lines, and creative use of color, in addition to the designs and the clarity of the images.

In the past, priests or members of the congregation learned the art within the vodou temple setting. Today, prominent artists pass the skill through apprenticeships in the secular environment of workshops.

Some of the Haitian master flag makers focus only on creating new designs and patterns, leaving the sewing to their assistants. Once proficient at sewing, apprentices move on to design, and later they open their own flag-making businesses.

Haitians are survivors. Living in the poorest country in the Western Hemisphere, victim to a large number of natural and social disasters, they are resourceful and quick to adapt. The constantly evolving central motifs on the vodou flags from the original African styles to the contemporary patterns reflect these qualities, as do the artists' responses to evolving markets. Many artists address market globalization by producing decorative art flags in addition to the

traditional vodou ceremonial flags. Secular buyers tend to focus on the quality of the work, and the beauty and originality of the design, rather than on the meaning and beliefs behind the patterns.

The motifs in flags that target these buyers, from tourists to international art dealers, are more varied than those in traditional flags. They often include designs that are not directly related to vodou, such as biblical scenes and images from popular culture.

Personally, I feel that paying attention to the story that accompanies a flag enriches the experience of purchasing and owning it. If you have the opportunity to visit Haiti, make your way to a flag maker's workshop or a vodou temple. Take the time to explore the artistry and history of these extraordinary works of art. When you finally decide which flag to purchase, you'll be buying more than a beautiful flag; you'll be buying a wonderful story too.

Resources

Cosentino, Donald. "The Lwa of Haiti."
    Hand/Eye Magazine, Fall–Winter 2010.
Frank, Priscilla. "The Hypnotic (and Very
    Glittery) Beauty of Haitian Vodou
    Flags." *Huffington Post*, October 1, 2014,
    huffingtonpost.com/2014/10/01/
    vodou-flag-_n_5909160.html.
Girouard, Tina. *Sequin Artists of Haiti*.
    Port-au-Prince, Haiti: Haiti Arts, 1996.
Padilla, Carmella. *The Work of Art—Folk
    Artists of the 21st Century*. Albuquerque:
    Museum of New Mexico Press, 2013.
Polk, Patrick Arthur. *Haitian Vodou Flags*.
    Jackson: University Press of
    Mississippi, 1997.
Smith, Clare Brett, ed. *Artisans of Haiti*.
    Photography and translation by Chantal
    Regnault. Washington, DC: Aid to
    Artisans, 2003.

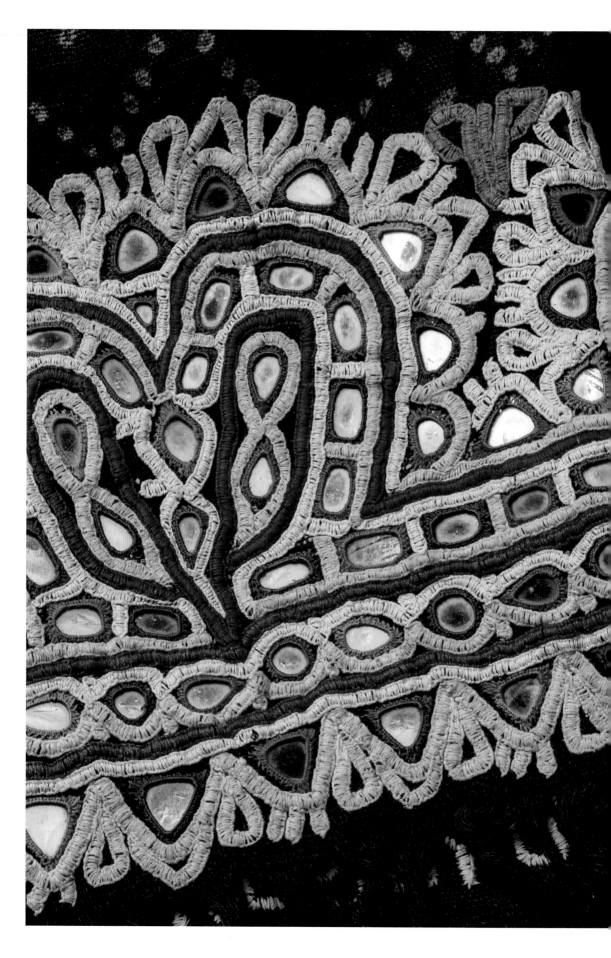

CHAPTER 19

India

Shisha Embroidery

A large cloud of dust kicked up by a herd of sheep is headed in your direction. You shade your eyes against the glare of the desert sun and peer through the haze, trying to identify the resplendent figures in the rear. They are clad in brilliant colors, accented with dazzling flashes of light.

As they approach, your suspicions are confirmed: you are in the presence of a Rabari family.

The nomadic Rabari roam the northwestern states of India, Gujarat and Rajasthan, in search of water and fodder for their herds of sheep, goats, cattle, and camels.

Rabari adults usually wear traditional dress, the turbaned men in white and the women in bright colors. Dense embroidery embellishes the women's shawls and blouses. Pieces of glittering mirror glass form mosaics within the bold designs.

Shisha is the Hindi word for mirror glass; the Muslims call it abla. Shisha embroidery, or mirrorwork, is a form of embroidery that incorporates small pieces of mirror glass.

The desert tribes, both Muslim and Hindu, believe that the mirrors, which represent the reflection of light on water, bring luck, prosperity, and fertility. They incorporate mirrorwork in their embroidery to ward off the evil eye by trapping it, reflecting it, or making it blink. Hence, in traditional pieces, the mirrors provide focal points within the embroidery, often as centers of flowers and the eyes of animals and birds. Mirrors also frequently border designs or divide patterns into sections.

Evidence suggests that shisha embroidery originated in the desert areas of the Indian subcontinent. It is a fundamental component of traditional needlework in Gujarat and Rajasthan in northwestern India and Sindh in Pakistan. It is also prevalent in the Deccan Plateau of southern India, in Afghanistan, and in eastern Sumatra.

The original source of reflective material was flakes of mica (a crystal) from the Sindh desert. European trading ships of the 1600s used shards of mirror glass as ballast, and with the increase in trade with Europe, mirror glass became readily available and started replacing the mica.

The traditional method of producing mirror glass for embroidery begins with large, thin-walled globes of blown glass, silvered on the inside. The globes are shattered into shards, which are cut with scissors into small shapes—roughly square, rectangular, circular, tear dropped, or triangular.

The production of hand-cut glass is still widespread in northwestern India, but mass-produced, machine-cut mirror glass is fast becoming the material of choice: it is less expensive and, being thicker, is not as fragile.

Since, unlike sequins, the mirrors have no holes in them, artisans attach them to the densely woven background fabric with stitches that frame and overlap the mirrors to hold the shisha in place, much like a picture frame holds a picture.

The groups who practice shisha embroidery include the Meghwal, the Memon, the Jat, the Rajput, and the Rabari. The embroidery of each ethnic group is usually clearly distinguishable.

The Meghwal, a Hindu caste of leatherworkers, embroider over block-printed cotton fabric, often using parts of the block-printed designs as outlines for the embroidery. They place circular pieces of mirror glass as integral parts of pictorial motifs and along selvedges.

The Muslim Memon are famous for their fine embroidery in floral designs. Their work includes tiny bits of mirror glass; some scattered in the background, others forming centers for the flowers.

Geometric designs characterize the embroidery of the Jat, seminomadic camel herders and breeders. They accent their abstract patterns with columns of large circular or pear-shaped shisha.

The needlework of Rajput, formerly a ruling caste, is dominated by square and diamond-shaped blocks. Interlacing latticelike patterns in yellow and white alternate with square pieces of mirror glass to form rows of repeats.

The Rabari combine mirror glass of different shapes in their work, fitting the shapes together like a tile mosaic, and stitching them in place with vividly colored thread.

The cloud of dust is upon you as the sheep and men amble past, but your red-rimmed eyes are drawn to the women bringing up the rear, riding high on camels. The mirrorwork on their blouses and shawls, designed to ward off the evil eye, proves its effectiveness by causing you to blink repeatedly as the mosaic of shisha reflects the sunlight.

Resources

Gillow, John, and Bryan Sentance. *World Textiles: A Visual Guide to Traditional Techniques.* New York: Thames & Hudson, 1999.

Leslie, Catherine Amoroso. *Needlework through History: An Encyclopedia.* Westport, CT: Greenwood, 2007.

Mahila, Maiwa, Kutch Mahila, and Vika Sangathan. *Through the Eye of a Needle: Stories from an Indian Desert.* Vancouver, BC: Maiwa Handprints, 2003.

Paine, Sheila. *Embroidery from India & Pakistan.* Seattle: University of Washington Press, 2001.

Paine, Sheila. *Embroidered Textiles.* New York: Thames & Hudson, 2010.

Willoughby, Janet. *Mirrorwork & Embroideries of Kutch.* DVD. Hampton, UK: Ends of the Earth, 2003.

CHAPTER 20

India

Bandhani

This was a completely new take on tie-dye for me.

I've done my fair share of quick and dirty starbursts, spirals, and stripes. There was nothing slapdash about bandhani. I stood in front of the display of bandhani shawls, completely bowled over. Though the bright colors were eye-catching—red, black, green, yellow, and blue—it was the tie-dye designs that drew me in for a closer look. It was clear that the intricate figurative and geometric designs made up of tiny resist-dyed dots, or bindi, were works of skilled artisans, products of days of intense labor.

Bandhana is a Sanskrit word meaning "to tie." It is also the origin of the English word for the kerchief that many of us use to absorb sweat from physical exertion—the bandanna.

The term *bandhani* refers both to the tie-dye technique and to the cloth itself, whether the resist dyeing produces fine dots, such as by the bandhani artisans of Rajasthan and Gujarat, or coarser circles, such as by the artists of Sindh and Mardhya Pradesh. The finer the ties, the more expensive the fabric.

The vast majority of bandhani artisans are members of the Khatri caste. The Khatri are a group of printers and dyers, both Muslim and Hindu, who work within family networks. Usually, the men do the dyeing in workshops and outsource the tying to women, who work from their homes to generate income without challenging societal norms.

To produce tiny dots in cotton or silk fabric, the women either use a small metal pick or grow their nails long to pinch and

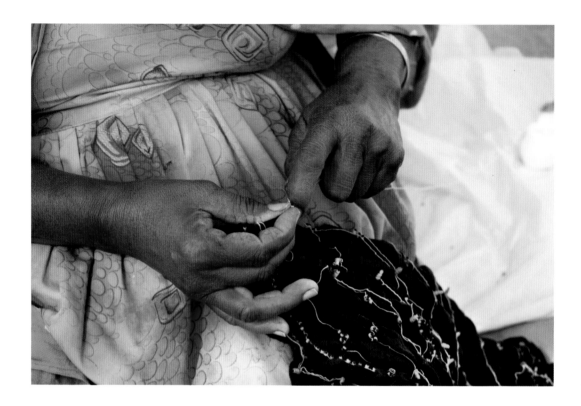

raise the cloth into small peaks, which they then wrap tightly several times with thread to form a bindi. When they work with heavier woolen fabric, they use their teeth to raise the tiny peaks. They tie the bindi in sequence without breaking the thread, so that after the Khatri men dye and dry the cloth, they can untie the knots easily in a single motion.

Before handing the fabric over to the women to tie, Khatri artisans stencil the overall designs on silk or light cotton cloth with a mixture of fugitive (temporary) dye and kerosene. For wool cloth, they mark the patterns with thread dipped in soot and kerosene. The women tie bindi along the lines of the designs, forming patterns that depict figurative motifs such as flowers, leaves, dancing girls, elephants, tigers, and birds, as well as geometric designs. Some bandhani pieces contain more than one size of bindi, most often a larger one forming a focal point for a pattern of smaller dots. More-complex designs involve submerging a single piece in several colored-dye baths, removing and adding ties in between dips, to create patterns in different colors.

Above & opposite, top: Photos courtesy of Prof. Ravi Poovaiah and Roopa Narayan Sahoo, D'source (E-kalpa Project)

Overall design is only one aspect that determines the quality of the craftsmanship. The uniformity of size and spacing and the shape of the dots are equally important. Square or diamond-shaped bindi are preferable to round or irregularly shaped ones.

Many residents of northwestern India prize bandhani work—saris, turbans, veil cloths, skirt lengths—for daily wear and for special occasions. The Rabari use woolen bandhani with a black background and yellow bindi for the women's veil cloths,

Bottom: Photo courtesy of Kamaldeep Kaur, Neelgar

which they embellish further with mirrorwork. And brides of affluent Gujarati families traditionally wear silk bandhani saris at their weddings.

I own several bandhani shawls: a red cotton shawl, with white bindi forming patterns of birds, leaves, and geometric shapes, and a Rabari shawl, where the yellow dots are part of a larger pattern that includes rich mirror embroidery. But my favorite bandhani piece is a simple silk indigo shawl that I dyed myself. Lacking the patience or skill (or long nails) to master the art of tying the knots, I bought a kit from Maiwa Handprints—a white silk shawl that had been hand-tied in the workshop of master bandhani artisan Aminaben Khatri from the Kutch Desert of India. After I finished dyeing and drying the shawl, I untied the first knot. The others followed in a magical and beautiful chain reaction.

Resources

Edwards, Eiluned. *Textiles and Dress of Gujarat*. London and Ahmedabad, India: V&A/Mapin, 2011.

Lynton, Linda. *The Sari: Styles, Patterns, History, Techniques*. New York: Thames & Hudson, 2002.

Ranjan, Aditi, and M. P. Ranjan, eds. *Handmade in India: A Geographic Encyclopedia of Indian Handicrafts*. New York: Abbeville, 2009.

CHAPTER 21

India

Laheria

"It was a very auspicious day—12/12/12. The day thousands of couples were getting married just in Jaipur alone. Who knows how many were marrying in India.

"As we headed to dinner a bit outside the main city, we could barely move as the wedding processions, led by a band, and grooms riding on elephants, clogged the streets. Cars inched along."

So wrote Marilyn about her adventures traveling with friends in India. They'd planned to visit a turban shop on their way to dinner but were unable to enter it due to the crowds.

Turban shops carry a variety of turbans, including plain, ajrakh, bandhani, and laheria.

Laheria (also spelled leheriya or leheria) is a resist dye technique unique to the state of Rajasthan in northwestern India.

The word *leher* means "wave" in Hindi, and the laheria patterns symbolize rain and bountiful harvest. The technique produces colorful patterns of diagonal stripes or zigzags across lengths of fabric. The fabric is used for saris, skirts, and shawls, as well as turbans.

Laheria artisans dampen thin fabric and roll it tightly on the diagonal, from one corner to the opposite corner, creating a tube. Moistening the fabric before rolling helps tighten the twist. When working with silk, to avoid damage to the delicate fabric in the binding process, the artisans first bandage the tube with thin cotton strips. Using thin permeable fabrics such as silk or cotton ensures dye penetration throughout the tube. This is also why laheria artisans typically use this method on turbans rather than larger textiles—the dye wouldn't penetrate the interior of thicker tubes made for sari lengths.

As in the bandhani method, the men are in charge of the dyeing and the women of the tying. The women follow precise instructions on the placement of the ties. To guarantee accuracy and to ensure that the ties act as resist throughout the compact tube, they tie the tube under tension by first securing it to a pole.

After dyeing the tubes, drying them, and removing the ties, the places where the ties were blocking the dye leave rings of undyed fabric. When the artisans unroll the fabric, the rings open up to reveal diagonal stripes across the fabric. The width and spacing of the ties determine the width of the stripes and their density.

There are several variations on the basic technique. Instead of rolling the fabric, some artisans fold it like an accordion across its width and then tie it, forming zigzags or wavy patterns instead of stripes.

Another option is mothra, where the artisans first apply the standard laheria technique, then unroll the dyed tube, reroll the striped fabric on the opposite diagonal, retie it, and dye it once more. Depending on the density of the ties, the resulting pattern can range anywhere from grain-like specks to larger squares or rectangles.

By successively untying, refolding or rolling, retying, and placing in different dye baths, the artisans add to the variety of patterns, creating stripes in different colors by using laheria or forming tartans using mothra. Additional variations include dip dyeing only parts of the tube or replacing one or more of the dye baths with a vat of bleach.

In rural areas, where traditional attire is still widespread, sari-clad women and men wearing turbans are a common sight on any given day. However, the more elaborate textiles, such as tie-dye turbans, block-printed saris, and ikat-woven shawls, make an appearance only on special occasions.

Turbans are an uncommon accessory in urban areas. But come their wedding day, most grooms across India haunt turban shops. They select their wedding turbans according to their caste and the time of year.

Photo courtesy of Kamaldeep Kaur, Neelgar

They have the staff in the shop tie it for them—in the cities, tying turbans has become a forgotten art.

Marilyn and her party found the turban shop packed, so they skipped the visit and went on to dinner. Upon telling their hostess of their adventures, including their disappointment over missing the turban shop, the hostess sent one of the staff down to the shop to procure an array of turban fabric.

Between dinner and dessert, Marilyn and her friends went out to the restaurant's courtyard and selected turban fabric. As a textile lover, I would consider looking through the fabrics *as* dessert!

Resources

Gillow, John, and Bryan Sentance. *World Textiles: A Visual Guide to Traditional Techniques*. New York: Thames & Hudson, 1999.

Murphy, Marilyn. Co-owner of ClothRoads, clothroads.com, and former president of Interweave Press, private communication, 2014–2017.

Ranjan, Aditi, and M. P. Ranjan, eds. *Handmade in India: A Geographic Encyclopedia of Indian Handicrafts*. New York: Abbeville, 2009.

Westfall, Carol. "Leheria." *Shuttle Spindle & Dyepot* 138 (Spring 2004): 43–49.

CHAPTER 22

Arabian Peninsula

Bedouin Weaving

Any reference to the Bedouin, the nomadic tribes who roam the deserts of the Arabian Peninsula, conjures up, in my mind, images of camel races across the desert, Arabian horses galloping on the sand, and the handwoven paired bags I bought when I was in high school. Smaller than camel saddlebags, I assumed they were donkey saddlebags. Slinging them over my shoulder, I used them to carry my books, thinking I was oh so cool, a trendsetter (despite the fact that no one picked up on the trend).

The origin of the term *bedouin* is the Arabic term *badawi* (plural *badu*), which means "desert dweller." The Bedouin are nomadic people, herders of camels, sheep, and goats. They are usually very clannish and have a clear hierarchy, based on their nomadic lifestyle. The camel herders consider themselves the elite, the most

authentic Bedouin—they can move quickly from pasture to pasture. And since camels can last months without water, their herders can spend long periods of time in the desert.

Next down in the hierarchy are the goat- and sheepherders, who have to move more slowly along routes that aren't too far from wells. The seminomadic people are lower yet in social rank; they roam the desert with their herds only part of the year. The rest of the time they remain in their villages farming. The lowest of the low are those who stay put, never wandering far from their home base.

Traditionally, the Bedouin relied on raiding and plundering for income. They considered war to be a noble activity that followed a code of honor. Reciprocal raids within a tribe and among neighbors and cousins were acceptable. Killing was

forbidden, as was taking noncombatants, including those who were asleep or unarmed. Tribal warfare was an equalizer, a way of spreading the wealth—the poor raided the rich.

The first king of Saudi Arabia, Abd al-Aziz, unified the tribes and outlawed tribal battles (other governments in the area followed his lead). Also, the discovery of oil in the 1930s brought prosperity to the region, eliminating the underlying reasons for intertribal wars.

Between bans on warfare, the discovery of oil, industrialization, the World Wars, and droughts, the Bedouin population declined markedly, and, with it, the nomadic lifestyle. Most Bedouin now live in settled communities. Yet, many of the traditions and customs prevail. In particular, handweaving continues to be central to the Bedouin daily life.

In the past, using handspun yarn, Bedouin women wove their tents, storage bags, saddlebags, cushions, and rugs. Nowadays, there's little need for handwoven tents, but the weavers still weave traditional items such as bags, rugs, and cushion covers for home use and for sale.

They still use handspun yarn, too, and the drop spindle remains the tool of choice. As their ancestors did before them, Bedouin women spin goat hair, sheep wool, camel hair, and camel down. The most-common yarn colors are the natural blacks, browns, tans, and white, as well as hand-dyed dark reds, orange, and blue. My saddlebags had a white background with lengthwise stripes of red, orange, and black.

    Photos courtesy of Joy Totah Hilden

Bedouin weavers use ground looms made of found materials. These looms are easy to transport when the tribe is on the move. The frame consists of four rods and four stakes. Two of the four rods form the front and back beams of the loom, a third rod is the heddle bar, and the fourth is the cross rod.

The weavers hammer the stakes into the ground to hold the front and back beams in place: two in front of the back beam, and two behind the front beam. The warp stretches along the ground between the beams. The stakes keep the beams from collapsing toward each other while maintaining an even tension on the warp.

It takes three women to warp a loom. The weaver sits at the front, or breast, beam, and another woman sits at the back beam. The third woman carries the ball of warp yarn back and forth between them, creating a figure eight on the way, which forms a cross between alternating warp threads. The weaver makes the decisions about the patterns, cutting and knotting together threads of different color when necessary. She winds each warp thread around the beam, passes it to the middle woman, who then takes it over to the woman at the back end, who, following the weaver's instructions, winds it around her beam and sends it back to the weaver.

The next step is to raise the heddle bar above the warp between the front beam and the cross by resting the bar on a pair of rocks or bricks. Like many indigenous weavers across the globe, Bedouin weavers loop yarn heddles over the heddle bar down to the warp to catch the threads from the upper half of the cross.

The final step in setting up the loom is to place the cross rod between the back beam and the cross, sliding it between the upper and lower warp threads to maintain the cross during the weaving process, to facilitate the formation of the shed and counter-shed. The placement of the cross defines the shed and counter-shed. When the cross lies behind the heddle bar, the gap between the (top) heddle threads and the bottom threads is the shed, where the weaver slides in the weft thread. When the cross is in front of the heddle bar, the non-heddle threads lie above the heddle threads, and the gap between them is the counter-shed. The act of weaving consists of repeatedly passing the weft thread through the shed and then through the counter-shed to produce plain weave (over-under).

The weaver's tools consist of one or more sword beaters to help open the sheds and beat down the woven part to make it denser, and a hook beater, either a metal hook or a gazelle horn, to beat down the weft in particular spots along the width of the piece. She also winds the weft yarn around various stick shuttles, which she uses to pass the weft back and forth through the sheds.

When she first starts weaving, the weaver sits on the ground in front of the loom. As the piece progresses, she moves to sit on the completed portion of the textile, moves the heddle assembly forward, and continues weaving. Unlike many other indigenous weavers in other countries, who move the heddle bar back and forth to open the sheds, Bedouin weavers move the cross back and forth, keeping the heddle bar stationary during the actual weaving process. The Bedouin weaver reaches behind the heddle bar and pushes and pulls on the warp threads to move the cross through the heddles.

Most Bedouin weaving is warp-faced plain weave, where the warp is so dense that it covers the weft, so that only the warp is visible in the finished product. The weaver creates designs by combining several colored yarns in the warp with various weft manipulations, including pick-up techniques. Some weavers further embellish their pieces by weft twining, which covers the warp, creating weft-faced sections.

I haven't had the opportunity to observe Bedouin weavers in action. I was delighted when I came across a group of Bedouin weavers from the Negev Desert in Israel during the 2012 Santa Fe International Folk Art Market. I searched their booth for a small set of saddlebags but was unsuccessful. Instead, I found a tasseled camel saddlebag woven in rich red and orange, deep blue and green, and the blackest of black. I bought a shoulder bag as well.

I'm still on the lookout for double saddlebags like those I had when I was a teenager.

Resources

Hecht, Ann. *The Art of the Loom: Weaving, Spinning & Dyeing across the World*. Seattle: University of Washington Press, 2001.

Hilden, Joy Totah. *Bedouin Weaving of Saudi Arabia and Its Neighbours*. London: Arabian Publishing, 2010.

CHAPTER 23

Bangladesh

Kantha Embroidery

One of my favorite haunts when I visited Boulder, Colorado, was a small fair-trade shop, Momentum. Whenever I popped in, I eyed the pile of kantha quilts hungrily, itching to buy one. But I always try to travel light, in terms of both luggage and budget, so, with great reluctance, I resisted.

The word *kantha* means "rags" in Sanskrit, a reference to the ancient Indian practice of recycling old fabric by remaking it into quilts. In the past, before the Industrial Revolution, kantha quilters made the quilts entirely from old dhotis, the traditional men's wear, an Indian version of pants, or from saris. They reused both the fabric and the thread they pulled from the fabric.

In the simplest kantha quilts, the stitches are merely functional, to hold the layers of cotton or silk fabric together. Running stitches stretch in straight, parallel lines along the entire length of the quilt.

The phrase "embroidered kantha" refers to more-ornate quilts, where needleworkers form patterns by sewing the multiple layers of fabric with parallel running stitches that encircle design elements, a technique that quilters refer to as echo quilting. They add detail to the designs with embroidery, using colored thread that in the past they pulled from sari borders.

Originally, kantha artisans were primarily from West Bengal and Bihar in northeastern India and from East Bengal, now Bangladesh, where the saris and dhotis were predominantly white. Perhaps this is the reason why in traditional kanthas, the background and thread were white.

In many of today's kantha pieces, the quilting thread is the same color as the background fabric, which accentuates the characteristic surface texture in the form of waves. Artisans create the wavy texture by stitching the layers together without pulling the fabric taut.

The embroidery in traditional quilts has a circular central motif, usually an open lotus blossom, representing purity and the center of creation. Stars, circles of interlocking hexagons, and concentric patterned rings are also common. The other basic element of a traditional kantha represents the tree of life, a symbol of fertility, which the quilter embroiders in each of the four corners of the quilt.

The corner trees, together with the central design, subdivide the quilt into quadrants. Each quadrant stands alone, containing a variety of patterns ranging from geometric designs to figurative images and pictorial narrative, forming an overall asymmetric design.

Most of the geometric patterns replicate ornamental sari borders. The narrative patterns can be historical or religious, though some tell stories from the quilters' daily lives. Common images include plants, fish, birds, people, and personal items. Images may have religious significance, such as representations of the goddess Lakshmi or of Vishnu's chariot. Some motifs represent qualities such as prosperity, growth, and harmony. Design elements that appear in pairs may have romantic or erotic connotations.

Before the industrialization of the region, needleworkers made kanthas for

winter quilts, covers, wraps, and ceremonial mats, typically keeping plainer ones for home use and saving more-ornate ones for gifts.

Kantha making went into a decline in the 1920s due to the Industrial Revolution but underwent a revival a few decades later in Bangladesh. Many of today's kantha quilts target the tourist industry and the global market and are made of new fabrics in the form of wall hangings, cushion covers, and other household items.

These days, the term *kantha* often refers to the style of embellishment rather than the quilting. The characteristic parallel running stitches are more ornamental than functional, and quilting plays less of a role. The background of most modern kantha pieces consists of no more than two layers of silk or cotton fabric, making them more cost-effective. Also, many of today's kantha artisans cut back on labor by embellishing their pieces only with straight, parallel running stitches, stretching across the length of the fabric.

A surprise package arrived in the mail a few weeks before I started writing this. Inside was a simple kantha quilt from Momentum, a gift from a good friend who shares my love of ethnic textiles. The requisite parallel stitching secures layers of old cotton saris, providing the lovely texture characteristic of kantha quilts. No embroidery other than the straight, parallel stitching embellishes the quilt; only the colorful pattern print on the soft worn fabric adds complexity to the textile, carrying stories I can only imagine.

Photos courtesy of Craft Revival Trust, India

Resources

Crabtree, Caroline, and Christine Shaw. *Quilting, Patchwork, & Applique: A World Guide*. New York: Thames & Hudson, 2007.

Gillow, John, and Nicholas Barnard. *Traditional Indian Textiles*. New York: Thames & Hudson, 1991.

Gillow, John, and Bryan Sentance, *World Textiles: A Visual Guide to Traditional Techniques*. New York: Thames & Hudson, 1999.

Mason, Darielle, ed. *Kantha: The Embroidered Quilts of Bengal*. Philadelphia: Philadelphia Museum of Art, 2010.

Newland, Judy. "Kantha: Ancient Hand Stitch Revival." *Clothroads* (blog), clothroads.com/kantha-ancient-hand-stitch-revival/.

Paine, Sheila. *Embroidery from India & Pakistan*. Seattle: University of Washington Press, 2001.

Ranjan, Aditi, and M. P. Ranjan, eds. *Handmade in India: A Geographic Encyclopedia of Indian Handicrafts*. New York: Abbeville, 2009.

Stevulak, Cathy, dir. and prod. *Threads: The Art and Life of Surayia Rahman*. Lakebay, WA: Kantha Productions, 2016.

CHAPTER 24

Spain

Espadrilles

When Imelda Marcos fled the Philippines in 1986, she was wearing a pair of black espadrilles. She had a collection of more than one thousand designer shoes to choose from. Why the espadrilles?

Espadrilles, simple fabric slip-on shoes with flexible jute soles, originated more than four thousand years ago among the peasants in the Pyrenees, the mountain range between France and Spain. The name *espadrille* comes from the French word *esparto*, the grass from which the original fiber craftsmen made the soles. Nowadays, the fiber of choice is jute, which is stronger than esparto.

The craft of making espadrilles by hand is still practiced in Spain. Traditional production consists of four steps; each step requires a specific skill that passes down from one generation to the next.

The only step that involves machinery is the first, where the artisan uses a spinning jenny to make rope out of jute fiber, which he then braids using a braiding machine.

In step two, the next artisan makes the soles, using a turntable to coil the braid tightly in the shape of a sole. The hardest part of his job is to sew the coils together with jute to prevent them from unraveling and to maintain the shape. Passing the needle back and forth through the coils across the width of sole requires both strength and dexterity.

A third artisan cuts two pieces for the uppers out of cotton canvas: one piece for the toe, another for the heel.

The only women involved in the process are seamstresses, whose job is to complete the last step in the process: sewing the uppers onto the rope sole with sturdy cotton thread, using a blanket stitch and adding extra reinforcement in the toe area.

Some espadrille makers add a fifth step to the process to fortify the sole. The traditional way of making the sole last longer was by coating it in tar. These days, it's treated with rubber.

The craft of attaching the canvas uppers by hand to the jute soles was widespread in Spain until the 1960s. Then espadrille machines in Asia started taking over, and the number of espadrille seamstresses steadily waned to near extinction.

Espadrilles came into vogue in the thirteenth century in Catalonia, in northeastern Spain, where they are still artisan made. In the early 1800s, the customer base expanded from the farming community to the military and clergy and, later, to the mining industry. In the late nineteenth century, espadrille makers started exporting the shoes to South America.

Another swell in demand occurred in the 1930s, during the Spanish Civil War, when both the Spanish military and the rebels wore espadrilles. The next big increase in production took place in the 1970s, when Yves Saint Laurent, the Parisian fashion designer, placed an order for wedge espadrilles, which became all the rage.

Traditional espadrilles were either black, which were worn on weekdays, or in the fabric's natural color, worn on Sundays. Modern espadrilles come in a wide range of fabrics and vary from a closed shoe to an open-toed sandal. They come in flat, wedge-shaped-heel, and platform models. Some sport ribbons to secure them to the wearer's ankles, similar to the ribbon wraps of ballet shoes.

Though there are many cheap imitations available in the global market, usually made in Asia, there is still a market for the authentic product. Despite being one of the oldest shoe designs in the world, espadrilles are still popular in their traditional form in France and Spain, perhaps in part because they are so comfortable. The jute sole, though tough, molds to the foot. Also, the jute soles and the cotton uppers allow the skin to breathe.

In the *New York Post* article about Imelda Marcos's shoe museum, there's a photo of her holding the pair of espadrilles that she wore when she fled her homeland. The shoes are open toed and have no laces. The heel is fairly low. They certainly looked a lot more comfortable than any of her designer shoes. They're definitely the shoes I would choose if I were fleeing for my life.

Resources

DeMello, Margo. *Feet and Footwear: A Cultural Encyclopedia*. Santa Barbara, CA: ABC-CLIO/Greenwood, 2009.

Espadrille Store. "History of the Espadrille." espadrillestore.com/en/the-history/.

"Neglect Ruins Imelda Marcos' Legendary Shoe Collection." *New York Post* (online edition), February 23, 2012, http://nypost.com/2012/09/23/neglect-ruins-imelda-marcos-legendary-shoe-collection/.

CHAPTER 25

Peru

Three-Dimensional Embroidery

Roaming around the WARP annual-meeting marketplace, I bypass the handwoven, natural-dyed bags from Bolivia—I already own two. Out of the corner of my eye, I spy colorful embroidery. Bugs? I step closer to the table and chuckle. They're ants, three-dimensional embroidered ants marching across handwoven cotton fabric, their bums up in the air.

Saturnino and Vilma Oncebay, representing the Oncebay family, brought to the US a collection of stunning textiles from Ayacucho, Peru. Fortunately for us textile aficionados, the WARP annual meeting was one of their stops on their trip.

The Oncebays are a family of textile artisans—spinners, natural dyers, weavers, and needleworkers. Members of the family have spent more than a decade studying Inca and pre-Inca textiles. Unlike the CTTC (Centro de Textiles Tradicionales del Cusco),

which focuses on revitalizing traditions that are close to extinction, the Oncebays, with Saturnino at the helm, work on replicating and reintroducing ancient techniques that have actually become extinct.

Vilma was responsible for the three-dimensional embroideries on the table. She based them on a two-thousand-year-old textile fragment the Oncebays found in a Chilean museum. The fragment held twelve lizards lined up head to tail along its length. Each lizard's torso, limbs, and tail were flat embroidered in a chevron pattern. The head, stitched to the torso, was three-dimensional and tilted upward, its nose in the air. According to Saturnino, the museum piece was from the Moche culture, which flourished on the northern coast of Peru from about 100 to 800 CE.

To incorporate the volumetric lizard heads and ant bums in her embroidery,

Vilma encloses seeds with thread, using embroidery techniques that date back to the Paracas culture, which reigned on the south coast of Peru from around 600 to 100 BCE.

She wraps embroidery thread around an elongated seed by using a variation on the chain stitch, which needleworkers refer to as cross-banding. In her work, as in the museum fragment, the cross-banding forms four equidistant braids running down the length of the seed, connecting the segments of thread (bands) that enclose the seed.

Replicating the lizards on the ancient textile fragment, she embellishes each lizard's head with eyes and a wide grin worthy of a crocodile. In the final step, she stitches the head onto the flat-embroidered torso.

As with other Oncebay textiles creations, the three-dimensional embroidered textiles are very much a family endeavor. The spinners in the family handspin alpaca fiber into fine thread, the colorists dye it with natural dyes, Saturnino weaves the background fabric, and Vilma does the needlework.

I bought two of Vilma's embroidery pieces: one with ants, the other with lizards. I can't help but chuckle whenever I see the line of marching ants. But the pair of lizards makes me laugh outright—they face each other, their volumetric heads almost touching nose to nose, crocodile smiles on their faces.

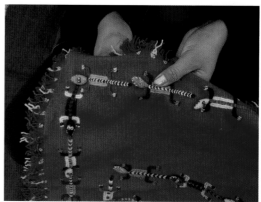

Resources

D'Harcourt, Raoul. *Textiles of Ancient Peru and Their Techniques*. Seattle: University of Washington Press, 1962.

Echavarria, Marcella. "Family Tradition." *Hand/Eye Magazine*, Summer 2012.

Pain, Sheila. *Embroidered Textiles*. New York: Thames & Hudson, 2008.

Pariona, Saturnino Oncebay, and Textil Oncebay, private communication, 2014–2017.

Wikipedia. "Moche Culture." https://en .wikipedia.org/wiki/Moche_ culture#Material_culture.

Wolff, Barbara. Professor of Anthropology, Montgomery College, Rockville, MD, private communication, 2014.

ABOUT WARP

Weave a Real Peace (WARP) began in 1992 when Deborah Chandler, author of *Learning to Weave*, contacted friends in the United States who were working with—or had an interest in working with—weavers and dyers in developing countries. Would they like to get together to share resources, provide support for one another, and exchange stories and experiences? The answer was a resounding yes! These first intrepid weavers gathered in the summer of that same year in Washington, DC, during Convergence, a biennial conference of the Handweaver's Guild of America, and a new organization was born.

WARP has stayed true its roots by providing networking opportunities to individuals and organizations working directly with community groups. It has grown to include all textile disciplines, including basketmaking, knitting, crochet, jewelry making, sewing, and many other craft media techniques.

In addition to linking members working in developing countries, WARP enables those who cannot work globally to become involved in supporting textile artisans worldwide. For more information, please visit the WARP website at weavearealpeace.org.

INDEX